FROM PA TO LA

FROM PA TO LA

from PITT to USC and beyond
the journeys of a small town jock

foreword by **Pete Carroll**

Thanks & Hail to Pitt

310-683-9888

YOGI ROTH

with Bob Bancroft

KMD
PUBLISHING, LLC.

2010 KMD PUBLISHING, LLC

Copyright © 2010 by Yogi Roth

Cover photograph by DeWalt Mix
Cover design by Brad Vinson
Interior text design by Sandy Janniche

All Rights Reserved.
No part of this book may be reproduced in any form or by any electronic
or mechanical means, including information storage and retrieval systems,
without permission in writing from the publisher, except by a reviewer
who may quote brief passages in a review.

Published by
KMD Publishing, LLC
841 E. Fort Ave, Suite 239
Baltimore, MD 21230

Reprinted by permission of KMD Publishing, LLC

ISBN-10 0-615-34807-6
ISBN-13 9780615348070

Printed in the United States of America

To those who have stood alongside me in my journey
And to those who have challenged me:

Thank you and I love you.

FOREWORD

It has been my good fortune to have met many extraordinary people in my life. I have been honored to visit with former presidents, talk with some of the most successful coaches that ever lived, and see an assortment of the greatest athletic competitors we have been so graced to watch perform.

In each of those individuals, regardless of their calling, I have seen a shared trait that I would describe as a willingness to be different, a unique burning desire inside that fueled them to surpass common expectation and normal landmarks without a moment's hesitation. They seem to hold onto uncompromising principles that lead them to achievements in their lives that separate them from the crowd.

Just two weeks before his passing, Coach John Wooden was describing his life's hero, his father. And in describing his father to my wife Glena and me, he simply said his father was an "unusual" man. It dawned on me at that moment that Coach Wooden could aptly be described as an "unusual" man himself.

These individuals have basically come from ordinary backgrounds, and their lives could have followed a path in a very common and ordinary manner. But along the way their lives turned in a direction of uncommon fashion. Not everyone faced with such opportunities and potential turns in the road of life chooses to follow the direction that leads them to separate from the norm.

It's an uncommon someone that senses the challenge and maybe the courage it takes to leave the path of certainty to the paths of uncertainty. I don't know if Coach Wooden would agree but I think there is an uncommon and an "unusual" nature in those that have risen above the crowd.

In this book, Yogi Roth demonstrates an incredible ability to look at a common upbringing from a most normal set of surroundings, and see extraordinary people and relationships that helped form one young man's life in a very extraordinary way. His vision and sensitivity for life's offerings have come together in this book to deliver a look at his life that comes straight from the heart. This work demonstrates a young man's zest for living his life to its fullest as he shares his childhood, his family, and his dreams with us in a most compelling journey. He takes us on a ride from an anywhere neighborhood in northeastern Pennsylvania, back in time to the shocking reality of a family's struggle to survive the Holocaust, and then forward to a young man's adventures in creating a career and a life in big-time sports and the world of entertainment in Los Angeles.

Yogi is one of those willing to separate from the crowd, willing to follow a path of uncertainty, and willing to travel in a direction that will lead him to live the life of an unusual man.

– *Pete Carroll*

PREFACE

I'M PATHETIC.

At least that's my opinion.

Yeah, straight-up pathetic.

Why? Well, a breakfast burrito changed my life. Not a six-figure offer, a significant raise, or a better title, but egg and melted cheese wrapped up in a flour tortilla. I mean, at least it could have been a smooth-talking blond recruiter who lied to me about my job description, a wanna-be LA promoter who told me his parties attract only A-list celebs, or a cute little old lady who tried to set me up with her gorgeous dogwalker who turned out to be a psycho, but no… nothing that cool.

Who knew that eating a breakfast burrito on a ratty old couch could have such power? A calorie-filled concoction that, only moments earlier, was wrapped in a truck by Armando's chorizo-stained hands. I mean, how could that alter my entire life?

But it did.

So, before you read another word, let's agree. I'm pathetic.

Oh, one more thing: along with that burrito came a voice of unbridled optimism and a winning sales pitch, which precipitated an insistent "Why not? Why not?" coming from somewhere deep in the left side of my chest.

Fast-forward four years, here I am coaching top-level college football, drawing pass plays, stapling practice scripts, chasing down dumb-ass freshmen, and having the best time of my life. Along the way, I earned a master's degree from the world-renowned Annenberg School of Communication, was a member of four straight Pac-10 championship staffs as well as four straight BCS bowl teams, worked with former and current NFL coaches, trained All-American athletes, attended the Heisman Trophy celebration, traveled to foreign countries, lived 100 feet from the Pacific, fell in love, fell out of love, developed a philosophy and approach to life, and made some of the greatest friends a person could ever ask for. So, first, really, I need to say this to the man who set this all in motion: thanks, Armando, that burrito was awesome. Hit the spot, man.

I was born and raised in the small, blue-collar town of Dalton, Pennsylvania. Geographically speaking, Dalton is 2,733 miles from Los Angeles, California. Figuratively speaking, Dalton and LA are further apart than Mars and Venus. In Dalton, football reigns, and a work ethic is not just a concept: it's a way of life for some 1400 people.

When I was a kid, my three friends and I would meet at 7:30 each morning on the corner of Main and North Turnpike. From there, we'd make our way to the Dalton Courts—the center of our young lives. We spent hours upon hours there playing hoops. And while our 8-year old minds believed that on those courts we invented the spin move, triple threat, meat-hook, and PR (Dalton slang for pick and roll), something more lasting emerged from that time: the foundation for a style, vision, theme, and philosophy was laid in each one of us. By not being allowed to call a foul, we discovered that nothing is given away in life. Through tough hand checks, we developed a competitive spirit. By learning how to go left, we understood that to be great we had to do things better than they had ever been done before. After being picked to play with the older kids, we realized that good things can happen to good people. And by clearing out the lane to go 1-on-1 for the game winner, we found out that hard work does pay off. The Dalton Courts became our mecca, where we could quench our competitive thirsts, fan the flames of our soon-to-be volatile social lives, and daydream about the many paths our futures might take.

And so it was on that rainy February morning in my new boss' office, on his beat-up orange couch over a wet burrito, that the lessons learned on the Dalton Courts met the *Win Forever* philosophy of University of Southern California football Coach Pete Carroll. A relationship was forged—coach and pupil, boogie-boarder and surfer, friend and friend.

As I wrap up this 2008-'09 season on the USC football staff, my final one, I feel compelled to reflect on the journey that brought me to this point. Not a direct route, nor an easy one, but its twists and turns have given me a life of extraordinary growth and change.

So, here goes: my path, my lessons learned, my story... from PA to LA.

PART I

from PA…

Main and North Turnpike

1

BEING A KID IN DALTON WAS EASY. Wake up, eat, run around, get dirty, run around some more, and finally come home. The worst part was when your mom took that 'Mom grip' and washed your hands. The water was usually too hot, the soap too soapy, and the coolness of being dirty faded in a matter of seconds. But for John Glenn, Nick Woody, Vince Walker, and me, the competitive spirit could not be washed away, for we found a way to turn any sport or game into a 2-on-2 match-up, from sunrise to sunset.

Ever since we were 5, we'd meet at the corner of Main and North Turnpike, rain or shine, ready to take on each other—and the world. These guys were my first team, my first crew, a bunch of rag-tag kids out in the sticks of Pennsylvania with nothing but active imaginations and boundless energy to carry us forward. Even though we'd be out of our parents' eyesight, we were never out of their earshot. How that little town survived us, I will never know.

Glenn was the natural athlete of the bunch (his dad and grandfather played for the Yankees, and his grandfather's claim to fame was that he caught the last game that Babe Ruth ever pitched). Tall, handsome, and funny, Glenn had a temper too—one day he was Zack Morris from *Saved by the Bell*, and the next he was borderline Dallas Winston from *The Outsiders*. The total jock, Glenn competed fiercely, took chances, and thrived on living on the edge. His older brother Chris, who would beat on him and his friends, was the superstar athlete in town. He could dunk, had a nasty jumper, and earned our complete admiration. We picked him for NBA stardom with the 76ers, but he ended up playing football at Penn State and remained our idol.

Glenn's sister Heather doubled as the first love of my life and my babysitter. The world couldn't have been any sweeter for an 8-year-old boy…well, except I had to face Heather in my one-piece PJs while she sat in our kitchen every other Thursday night doing algebra homework, wearing Britney Spears schoolgirl plaid.

Woody was the intelligent one—a future Congressman with a determined small-town work ethic. He got straight A's without trying, great SAT scores without studying, and the admiration of all our teachers without sucking up. Add to that, he was a multi-talented athlete who could shoot, dribble, and defend. We described him as a combination of Bill Bradley, 'Pistol' Pete Maravitch, and good ol' Albert Einstein. Yet with that came a price. He sunburned easily, had no dance skills, and faced constant heckling from Glenn because he had red hair and freckles. He was pretty funny too, but the Woody sense of humor reminded us of our tongues after eating seven saltine crackers in a minute—dry.

Woody was also the lover of our group. In sixth grade, we would ask him to tell us stories about his ladies. Not because none of us could get a date, but because he was helping himself to Glenn's red Diamondback Sorrento bike and pedaling over to Elena Bush's, where, we heard, he rounded second base. In the meantime we were still stealing our dads' cologne and pretending to shave while dreaming about just making it to first with Woody's girlfriend.

How do I describe Vince? The perfect one who could not hurt a fly, he still scared the daylights out of Glenn, Woody, and me. Athletic, big-boned, and competitive, Vince knew only one way to succeed in life—to outwork his opponent. Yet he too had another side to him: he was jovial, charming, and a *complete* ass-kisser. But as sick as it makes me feel to admit this, Vince actually meant everything he said. He really did care how Woody's Aunt Lori was doing in nursing school, he truly thought about Glenn's Uncle Joe in Jersey (whom Vince had met once), and he desperately yearned to know how well my dad was doing splitting logs for the winter's firewood. Ass-kisser, or legit? The jury is still out.

Vince could also u-turn from being the sweetest guy in town to being the most intimidating competitor around. Come game time, Vince didn't care who you were or where you came from. He'd get that look in his eyes—a squinty look, because he had small but very fiery eyes. He shot the ball relentlessly due to his firm belief that he could make every jumper he took, including the self-invented meat-hook, which is still unstoppable. Pure at heart and the nicest guy in town, Vince was the one we all cheered for. By the time we were 10, we knew he would be Prom King, and by the time he was 18, he had the crown to prove it.

As kids, the four of us experienced everything together—jubilation, heartache, teamwork, and youthful indiscretion. At 11, we tasted our first beer, two cans of Budweiser in the attic of my garage, while we gawked at a *Playboy* that Glenn had stolen from the Dalton Lumber Yard. The four of us had just finished playing the Dalton Wiffle Ball League Championship Series, in which the Mariners (Vince and I) defeated the Yankees (Glenn and Woody) in game seven. In our minds, we, like any World Series champions, earned those two horrible-tasting Buds.

From this stellar start, we moved to our first "older kids' party" in fifth grade. Glenn and I sported khaki shorts, button-down short-sleeved shirts, and Docksiders with no socks and the laces curled up. A memorable evening: I got my first French kiss. It was from Jen Suprick, a sixth-grader, as "When I Look into Your Eyes" by Firehouse rocked the house.

At 12, we enjoyed our first ride around the block after I borrowed (okay, stole) my Dad's Volvo while he was at work, and we jammed out to 2-Pac.

And who could forget 13 and our first time meeting blackberry brandy and Canadian whisky at Glenn's? We downed shot after shot, we acted like a bunch of fools, and by the end of the evening, we had perfected the art of upchucking. Nice work.

At 16, we all approached serious girlfriend time. Dior, the extremely attractive head cheerleader from the rival high school, starred as the love of my life: we were going to get married and have four kids, while changing the world together for the next 50 years. Glenn was about to have Jen Suprick's (yes, the same Jen Suprick) name tattooed on his arm, Woody was simultaneously managing his application to Harvard and an energetic girlfriend, while Vince took a different gal on a movie date every Saturday night.

Through it all, Glenn, Woody, Vince, and I thought we were so cool—way cooler than reality no doubt indicated. But we had a childhood that many kids around the world would envy, as we developed friendships and created lasting memories via the Dalton Courts.

On that asphalt we also taught one another that nothing in life comes without hard work, and that one cannot choose when to compete. That daily trek to and from the corner of Main and North Turnpike nurtured and molded each one of us as we began to understand who we were and what we stood for.

While I know I haven't yet grasped the full meaning of those days, I can tell you that our childhoods were a recipe for success. Today, each of us remains a competitor, and we all are successful, according not only to society's standards, but also to our own value systems. And most important, we've remained the best of friends since those early days on the Dalton Courts.

But our foursome was often more than just us four: Ravi, my younger brother was always included. Three years younger than we were, he was often a step slower or a few minutes late, but he was my brother and was always part of the group.

Ever since he was little, Ravi had both a passion for hanging out with us and a growing need for independence. At first he'd just watch our 2-on-2 battles, but as time passed, he would stray off on his own, sometimes playing with other kids, other times lying on the grass lost in his imagination, staring at the clouds. I never really noticed it too much, mostly because I only wanted him there to rebound for me after the games ended, or to walk home with me under the streetlights. Without him knowing it, though, he played, and continues to play, a vital role in my life: he drives me to perform.

Ravi may have followed in my footsteps—Little League, basketball, even some football (as my tackling dummy)—but then he took it a step further. After our day of athletics was done, he kept going. Performance, for him, meant films, plays, characters, roles.

So while I was bounding over garbage cans in my Strength Shoes, trying to become Jerry Rice, Ravi was perfecting his craft as an actor. His performances were unconfined by the boundaries of the athletic field or by the rules of the game. He had no limits when he was on stage.

He joined the Church Mouse Players, a group that met in a small playhouse in a neighboring town. Cast as the lead in nearly every production, he'd bounce easily from the basketball court or the baseball diamond to the stage. And our backyard was his rehearsal studio. Though I told myself that Ravi was following my path, and our sister Maya, also a performer, believed he was echoing her, the truth is that Ravi was far out ahead of both of us.

He had to have seen the irony. Here I was, his big brother, and I began to audition for the same plays, practice the same piano songs, and even try to belt out lines on cue when no one was listening. But for some reason I could never work my way up to what Ravi did so easily. He was clean and clear, a natural. I was never jealous of that, but I was fascinated.

One time we both auditioned for *Aesop's Fables*, and since the role I longed for was that of a sheep who apparently sang (don't ask), I practiced "La Bamba" obsessively all week. I got there prepared to bring the house down. I was psyched. I was pumped. I was ready. Then I hopped up on that four-foot high stage and felt like I was way up on top of a mountain somewhere. When the accompanist began to play, the notes sounded as if they were coming from miles away. I opened my mouth. Silence. The accompanist started again. And I croaked out "La, La, La…" before I ran out of breath. Again the opening notes. I'd get it this time, I knew it. "La, La, Lllll…." Even less than try number two.

For my fourth and undoubtedly triumphant whack at the song that Ritchie Valens made famous, I relaxed, focused, and then just froze. Just stood there. Silent. Finally, the casting director, Jane Honchell, threw me a lifeline. "Yogi, why don't you just sing Happy Birthday?"

Humiliated, I nodded, and sang the easiest song in the world ever so quietly.

As I walked off the stage and toward the back of the room, it wasn't my mom or sister who spoke first, but the kid who had been tagging along with my friends and me for the past seven years. We looked at each other, and he smiled and asked, "Hey, Yog, want to shoot some hoops when we get home?"

As we drove home my embarrassment turned to anger. Not at Jane, Ravi, or the accompanist, but at myself. How could I not perform when the lights were on? How could I not step up to the plate? How could I freeze when asked to take the game-winning jumper from the top of the key? After we pulled into the driveway and tumbled out of our green Beetle, Ravi got the basketball and turned on the garage lights. For two hours I shot, dribbled, and worked on my spin move, and for two hours Ravi wordlessly rebounded.

Finally, when Mom called us in, he and I walked up our driveway, stride for stride, and into the house. Knowing what went down that day, how I felt, and how her baby boy helped me, Mom greeted our sweaty, dirty bodies and tousled hair with one sentence: "Boys, remember, there are no small roles, only small actors."

That night I realized something. I was lying in bed, shooting a basketball up in the air, endlessly, and Ravi was lying in his bed, and I thought about how different we were, yet how much the same. My world would never only be about the championship teams I was on, just as Ravi's would never only be about the terrific roles he got. No, our lives would be about the performing itself. And the moments that would shape us would be those times when we would be counted on to lead our teams or our casts—and Ravi and I had to learn from these moments, whether we were together or apart.

Oh, and by the way, Mom was wrong. There are small roles. I got one. Third Sheep in *Aesop's Fables*. Ravi got the lead.

EARTH SCIENCE

2

Knowledge is no burden to carry. – Will Roth

"YOGI! YOGIIIIII! HOP IN THE CAR!" I heard that holler so many times when I was a kid.

You try growing up in small town America with a name like Yogi. First of all, you can never pretend you didn't hear it. And on a deeper level, at least from my parents' perspective, the name "Yogi" says there's a great big world out there, way more than what you see right in front of you, and it tends to set you on your own unique path as you explore that world. Maybe my parents had some sort of plan.

In any case, they didn't stop with the name thing—Mom and Dad did whatever they could to expand my horizons. Karate was a no-brainer. But this also meant guitar and piano lessons—Ravi and Maya were both musically inclined and eager for training, so my parents may have figured, why not toss the middle kid's muddy, grass-stained body into the back seat along with them? On the other hand, maybe there was that master plan.

I didn't last long at piano or guitar—too much sitting. Karate, though, kept my interest for a while, and combined with the music lessons, taught me the power of discipline. By learning to read music and by practicing Kata #1, I discovered how to focus. By rehearsing my scales, I found out how important it is to prepare completely. After watching Tom Hanks in *BIG* and desperately wanting to play "Heart and Soul" as well as he did, I understood the value of constant practice. And when I watched the glowing faces of my brother and sister as they played Mozart and Bach in front of several hundred people, I finally appreciated the power of the trained brain. Football, basketball, and baseball eventually took over my life, but it was karate, guitar and piano that built the strong mental foundation that underlies my athletic career.

My parents, Devorah and Will, met at 18 on a blind date. From rival high schools in northeastern Pennsylvania, they attended Syracuse together, backpacked through Europe and the Middle East at 22, and protested the Vietnam War in the Sixties. They may have looked like long-haired hippies (I've seen the photos), but they were clearly wise beyond their years in a spiritual sense.

Mom was born in Haifa, a beautiful seaside city in northern Israel near the Lebanese border—but left for Germany with her family when she was 5, where they lived in a refugee camp for several years until they could finally emigrate to the U.S. When her feet hit American soil, she realized instantly that the United States of America is beyond doubt the land of opportunity. She cemented that singular thought in her children's minds, but in an unorthodox fashion, at least for the times. Though she praised achievement, she always set the bar higher after each new challenge was met. "I'm not your best friend," she'd say, "I'm your mom." Though she could never conceal the twinkle in her eye when she said it.

Not to say that she wasn't tough—she is, in every sense of the word. Highly competitive, she does not accept losing, period; she has a fiery passion for everything she undertakes. But it was her firm and not always subtle display of emotion about drive and determination that made the deepest impression on all of us. She wasn't as concerned with our winning everything or performing brilliantly as she was with our participating totally and fearlessly. It was evident from day one that half-hearted effort would not be tolerated in our home. We knew that if we didn't take advantage of the life we had been offered, we were failing not only her, but more importantly, ourselves. You could say that Mom feels things deeply, passionately, and has a gift for communicating that.

Although she stayed home and raised us kids until Ravi was 12, she never stopped learning. When she was earning her master's degree in art therapy, she made certain that we saw how hard she worked to learn new things, and how much she valued the opportunity for continual and advanced education that this country provides. Ultimately, Mom taught us to dream impossible dreams and to dare to be great.

I think she inherited this mind-set from her parents, Holocaust survivors who had fled Europe for Israel, and then finally had found home in Scranton, Pennsylvania. We'd visit them often, and always on Jewish holidays, which I admit were somewhat of a mystery to me as a kid. I never really understood the significance of each particular holiday, but I always knew when one was coming up—the single pair of nice pants I owned would be laid out on my bed, hard shoes at its foot. I'd always try to get out of the event for a game of hoops at the Dalton Courts, but it never worked. So I'd swap my sneaks for the penny loafers and stare at the clouds on the endless twelve-mile trip into Scranton, while I plotted my path to NBA stardom.

The religious rituals changed with each holiday, but my behavior didn't. I'd go out in my grandparents' yard and pick weeds for a while, then I'd climb their one tree, and then I'd beat on my little brother until dinnertime. The meal varied with the seasons and with the particular religious event being commemorated, but invariably, after dinner, Baba and Zayde (that's Yiddish for Grandma and Grandpa) would sit us down and tell stories.

And what stories they were. I'd just stay there spellbound, listening as they transported themselves back in time, across the ocean to Poland and Israel, even as they remained right there across from me in their orange dining room chairs. They'd mix the Yiddish with English, their eyes would well up, and then Mom and Baba would start clearing the table, trying to conceal their tears from Ravi, Maya, and me. They'd clean everything off that white tablecloth except my turquoise glass, half-filled with ice and Crystal Club ginger ale. Amazing how I can still remember that glass, and how cold it felt in my hand, and how I was unable to move a muscle, as I sat transfixed by Zayde, who seemed to be lost, far away in the Warsaw ghetto.

Their stories of the Holocaust and the Nazis were epic, in every sense of the word—long, perilous, heroic, and ultimately, triumphant. Even when I was just 8 or so, I realized my grandparents' strength was something far out of the ordinary.

Once, when Baba was walking home from grammar school, her teacher stopped her short of her house and said, "You can't go home."

"Why not?" Baba asked.

"Your family has been axed to death."

From that point on, Baba was on the run, hiding in farmhouses far from the villages. Whenever she was asked, she said she was Christian, yet in her heart she prayed the war would end, the Germans would be defeated, and that she could tell the truth about who she was. The entire war, Baba was never captured by the Nazis. On one occasion near the final months of the Holocaust, she snuck into town to witness a local hanging. To her horror, the man being hanged was her cousin.

As dramatic as Baba's story was, it was matched in impact by the exploits of Zayde. A talented soccer player, he competed against the best in Poland. And then came the war and the Holocaust, and every Jew's life was changed forever. In Zayde's own words, from a letter he wrote to Simon Wiesenthal when I was a teenager:

> *My name is Morris Fish, I'm seventy-seven years old, and I want the world to know what I did in my young age. I keep this in secret in me, but I want to take it out from me because I can't keep it no longer. Too much pain.*
>
> *I'm a survivor from two concentration camps, Dachau and Majdanek. In 1943 the Gestapo took three hundred men from Dachau and shot us in the grave and left us to die. I was shot eight times. With my will to live I survived. I myself, and a general from Russia, and a professor from Poland. When night came we were still alive. We left the grave and after about a kilometer we saw a house, and came to the house. There was a German woman who took care of me. We stayed the night and left in the morning. Going through the woods three nights and three days, I fell. I couldn't go on because of weakness and no food and loss of blood from gunshot wounds. My friends helped me about a half a mile. We met up with the Partisans.*

His story continues, as Zayde, in his early 20s, joined the Partisans, the Jewish resistance movement. Some twenty to thirty thousand strong, they hid in the forests of Poland and Germany and survived on stolen or smuggled food. Most, like my grandfather, were young men in their teens and 20s, and their mission was to sabotage the Nazis by targeting supply trains, power plants, and so forth. As armed guerilla fighters, they also organized resistance within the Jewish ghettos throughout Eastern Europe.

Zayde fought in the most well-known resistance event, the Warsaw Ghetto uprising, side by side with Mordechai Anielewich, their brave 24-year old leader. He was one of the few who survived this infamous battle, in which the Nazis set fire to the homes, and then guarded the escape routes with machine guns. Many tens of thousands died, yet Zayde somehow escaped into the forest once again, and stayed with the resistance until the war ended. Then he came out of hiding, married a young beautiful woman named Regina, with whom he had a young son, Abram.

July 4, 1946 was a day the family eagerly anticipated—it was Zayde's birthday, his first with his new child. The war was over, the Holocaust ended. Zayde and his new family were alive, safe, living in the open with other Jews in Kielce, Poland. It should have been a day of celebration and thanks. But that was not to be.

On that shameful date, following a false report of a Polish boy kidnapped by gypsies or Jews (it never happened, and that is accepted fact today), a mob of Kielce townsfolk attacked every Jew they could find. Forty two died, most beaten to death by the mob, soldiers and police; Zayde's young wife was shot by police "while trying to escape." They shot the baby too. He was three weeks old.

This pogrom, arguably the most heartbreaking in Polish history—the war was over, millions of Jews had died, and yet the hatred persisted—precipitated the emigration of many Jews from Poland to Israel. Zayde was among them, as was my Baba. They met, shared their stories, and took the first steps toward sharing the rest of their lives together.

This family history they brought to us, however tragic, always resonated with life, happiness, and most importantly, love. Their struggle to survive, already embedded into my mother's life philosophy, became etched into my own heart more indelibly with each passing holiday.

Yet Baba, no matter how involved she was in retelling her stories, always had time for that special moment with each of her grandkids. It was sort of a ritual, different for each one of us, and I've remembered it always. She would ask, "How's your girlfriend?" to which I always shyly mumbled, "Um, I dunno...which one?" And she always laughed. To Baba, who had lost so much, family and connection were everything.

My parents would agree. Mom and Dad were both social workers making $11,000 per year combined when they had Maya, the eldest and smartest, then me, the jock, and finally Ravi, the actor. With three fast-growing kids sitting around the dinner table each night, Dad took a hard look at the family finances, and realized that a change was in order. So Dad followed the path he knew best—his own father's.

His dad, also named Will, was a World War II vet. His last assignment was to liberate Nazi war camps—and as he walked people out the camps, he carried with him photos of the stacks of bodies, to remind himself of what had happened and why he was a soldier. He came home to spend 17 years in the coalmines of Pennsylvania—and then one day he just quit, to start his own business in hardware and tool design. "Do what you love, and love what you do," he would say. Grammy Roth was his match in every way, a highly educated, strict, no-nonsense church-going community activist—and her motto was, "Never stop learning."

As a child, Dad would watch his father hop from chair to couch reading everything from the Bible to the *Encyclopedia Britannica*, and a variety of literary works in between. Grampsy had an unquenchable thirst for knowledge, and he never concealed this from his young and inquisitive son. Dad inherited that same curiosity about life and the world around him, and built upon it.

So my dad taught himself to be a stockbroker. When you're a broker, he tells me, your salary is dependent on what you sell, not how many hours you work. And Grampsy had encouraged this choice years before, when Dad was 12: he taught my father how to buy his first stock.

Dad was, and may still be, ahead of his time. A free spirit, he snuck his first beer at 12, partied, and dated the cool chicks. He went to the Pennsylvania state championships in wrestling and was a relentless linebacker who hit opponents so hard that he sent himself into a coma during his junior season. As a result, Dad walked away from football prior to his senior year and was still voted team captain. A man to admire.

Dad, though, is kind of free with the advice, I must say. I've heard plenty of it my whole life. At first, I thought his aphorisms were just a bunch of words in italics, but when they finally penetrated my hard head, they also shaped me and the people around me. It's amazing how one simple thought from father to son can have an impact far beyond the immediate. It's also clear where he got this ability to shape life's lessons into hard-to-forget phrases: his own parents.

After I received my master's degree from USC, I sent my thesis to legendary UCLA basketball coach John Wooden. The basis of my thesis was to find those elements that make a great coach an extraordinary one. Coach Wooden, Coach Pete Carroll of USC, and Duke basketball coach Mike Krzyzewski were the subjects of my study, and it was my mission to read about them, interview or attempt to interview them, and ultimately uncover what they had in common.

As a child, Coach Wooden was very close to his father, Joshua, an Indiana farmer and a strong disciplinarian. With love and wisdom bonding the two of them, according to his books, Coach Wooden lived his life to please his father and make him proud. What he remembered most about his dad were his "Two Sets of Threes" and his "Seven Things to Do" creed: "My father had what he called his 'two sets of threes.' They were direct and simple rules aimed at how he felt we [his sons] should conduct ourselves in life. The first set was about honesty: Never lie, Never cheat, Never steal. The second set was about dealing with adversity: Don't whine, Don't complain, Don't make excuses." As Wooden grew up, he kept those lessons close to his heart. When he graduated from grade school, he received his second lesson from his father, this time on the back of a business card. "At the top of the paper," Wooden recalls, "It said 'Seven Things to Do.'" It read as follows:

1. *Be true to yourself.*
2. *Help others.*
3. *Make each day your masterpiece.*
4. *Drink deeply from good books, especially the Bible.*
5. *Make friendship a fine art.*
6. *Build a shelter against a rainy day.*
7. *Pray for guidance and count and give thanks for your blessings every day.*

All his dad said when giving Wooden the card was, "Son, try and live up to these things."

Now, my Dad has never been a famous head coach, though he probably would have been a great one. But he too has lived by a set of principles, and has left me many notes with life lessons inscribed on them. Along with my thesis, I sent Coach Wooden a compilation of my father's phrases:

My Father: A Great Leader, a Constant Learner, a Lifelong Educator

- *Be curious.*
- *Always keep learning.*
- *To thine own self be true.*
- *The truth will set you free.*
- *Life is nothing without love.*
- *You are the company you keep.*
- *Live a life with purity & focus.*
- *Knowledge is no burden to carry.*
- *A penny saved is a penny earned.*
- *A fool and his money are soon parted.*
- *Everybody is a nobody and a somebody.*
- *You'll have either time or money, not both.*
- *At the end of the day, greatness is defined by each individual.*
- *Love many, trust few, and always remember to paddle your own canoe.*

After reading them, Coach Wooden sent me a note:

For Yogi—with best wishes. Those are wonderful words from father to son.
— John Wooden

This advice is now more ingrained in my head than throwing the slant off of a three-step drop. And one of the greatest lessons I have ever learned came from my dad's wisdom, patience, and restraint. When I was in seventh grade, I came home from school with a progress report from Mr. Rupp: I was failing his Earth Science class. Failing. For Mom, I might as well have maimed the sweet lady next door who worked at the Dalton Post Office. She was just a little upset.

For Dad, it was different. He sat me down, and we talked it over.

"Dad, I hate earth science. I mean, when am I ever going to need to know what a gymnosperm is? I just don't care."

Dad sat quietly at the foot of my bed, and when he spoke, it was kind of man-to-man, in a way. "Son, yes, I agree," he said. "You may never need to know about gymnosperms. But will it really hurt you to learn about them?"

I shook my head. The same head that was on the verge of failing seventh grade.

Then Dad looked me straight in the eye and offered one more thing.

"Yogi, knowledge is no burden to carry."

LOOKING UP

3

MOM AND DAD WERE TOUGH ACTS TO FOLLOW—to say nothing of Baba and Zayde. All three of us kids felt like we had mountains to climb before we could reach their heights. But because of their life experiences, they made sure we appreciated the importance of family unity, and how it could help us reach our dreams. We were always there for each other, no matter what—Maya for us two boys, Ravi and I for each other and for her.

Maya ranks first by birth, but also by brains. Easily the smartest of us three, she's also the most competitive, believe it or not. Whatever she does, she has to do it better (and faster) than it's ever been done before. She taught me how to hate girls, love girls, get over girls. She also taught me how to write, and how to stay authentic and true to myself no matter what I do. And her most lasting gift to me is the one that guides me day by day: life, she said, is about teaching, and that's how you change society, one mind at a time.

Fresh out of Ithaca College, she moved to Harlem at 21, English degree in hand, to teach her first class. Pick any 13-year old out of that group, and you'd be guaranteed they had dealt with more in their short existence than she had growing up in Dalton. And her first two years she had plenty to handle—she was stalked by some psycho and mugged twice, yet she refused to be intimidated. Instead, she rose to the challenge that the Big Apple threw at her, and got her master's degree from New York University and her doctorate from Columbia. Now she's the young principal of a charter school in Brooklyn. She walks the walk.

Not that she presents the picture of the overachieving academic. Hardly. This is a girl who snorts when she laughs, after all, and she laughs a lot. Though her obsession with Scrabble is something I consider almost dangerous, she also really likes to cut loose, and says, in her own lingo, that she "can't deal with people who are *el serioso* all the time." In constant motion, she's apt to be at spin class at dawn and Bikram yoga at dusk. Cap that off with late-night dancing to Fleetwood Mac and Missy "Misdemeanor" Elliott, Maya is just plain full of life. Her friends say she needs to stop trying to save the world, and the kids of the next generation. Her response: "Naïve? Maybe. Optimistic? Definitely."

If Maya is the high-spirited intellectual of the family, and I'm the jock who lives sports 24/7, then Ravi is the entertainer with the energy that would never cease to astonish you. First were the live performances in the backyard, then leads in all the school plays, and now, a career in New York theater. My little bro has been performing since he could walk.

He certainly didn't choose an easy path. Acting is definitely as competitive as any professional sport, because the gigs are few and the out-of-work actors are many. Ravi has been lucky, but many close friends and former classmates have been luckier—many are working steadily, some on Broadway, some in Hollywood. No matter whether he's just auditioning, doing a few lines on a soap opera, or working in a show off-Broadway, Ravi celebrates their more front-and-center successes whole-heartedly. He trusts that his hard work will pay off and that his time will come. And it will.

I love watching him sing, dance, act—whatever he does, I'm there to see it, whenever I can. But one moment stands out above all others, and it happened off-stage, not on.

It was January 3, 2003, the night that Ohio State beat Miami in overtime for the National Championship. A junior at Pitt, I had played a decent amount and even had started as a wide receiver here and there. And six weeks earlier in the season our team had lost to Miami on the final play—on an incompletion. It haunts me to this day. Had my arms been just a few inches longer, or the pass just a bit shorter, alums have told me I'd be a statue at the University of Pittsburgh right now. So watching the Buckeyes and Canes compete for a trophy that nearly was ours was pretty unappealing to me, and Ravi knew it. Yet I had to watch.

I was in my dad's home office randomly checking e-mail at halftime, when Ravi bolted into the room. He plopped himself down, all nervous energy, and waited for me to look away from the screen. Finally he asked me if we could talk. "Sure, " I said, "What's up?" He was on winter break from his freshman year at the Boston Conservatory of Music, and at first I figured it was some not too deep question about dorm life, or class work, or something.

But he seemed a little intense for that. "Yogi, I have something to tell you...."

"What's the problem?" I asked.

He blinked rapidly; a tear fell to his cheek. "I'm not sure how to say it...." He looked at the floor and wiped his eyes. I had never seen him quite so worked up.

"What're you, cryin'?" I tried to joke away the tension in the room but failed miserably.

"I have to tell you something."

"Uh, okay, Rav," I said tentatively, while mentally flipping through the many troubles that first-year students can encounter—was it drugs, was it bad grades, was he getting kicked out of school? What could it be? I prepared myself for the worst. "Just go ahead."

Ravi turned away, and thirty long seconds passed—during which I relived our entire lives together.

Finally he spoke. "Yogi, I know you may be mad at me and that's ok but... I can't help it and...if you don't want to talk to me...if you want to beat me up, I...."

"Ravi, what is it, man? Spit it out!" Now it was full-on tears. The lump in my throat tripled in size. Oh, man, I thought, this is bad.

Another long pause. This was getting intolerable.

"Yogi..."

Pause.

"I'm gay."

I didn't even take time to think. I just blurted, probably kind of loudly, "That's it? You're gay? How could you be afraid to tell me? We're brothers and—how could you think—"Then I stopped. I needed to just shut up for a sec. To take this in.

Now it was my turn to take an agonizing pause. Finally I said, slowly and quietly, "We're brothers. I love you. You're gay. I don't care. I love you. You're my brother. And if anyone looks at you wrong or says anything negative, let me know. I'll kick the shit outta them."

He was so relieved. I will never forget that. Some monumental weight was lifted from his shoulders, and he stood up. It was a great moment between us.

Yet the minute he left the room, I turned on myself. I slouched back in my chair, dropped my head, and stared blindly at the 17-inch PC screen as random instant messages popped up from college friends on winter break. My thoughts were a jumble. I was so proud of Ravi, but I have to admit, ashamed of myself. Ashamed that my brother, my best friend, was scared to tell me he was gay. Ashamed that he was nervous about talking to me, his older brother. Ashamed that I had used words like 'gay' and 'fag' in the locker room without hesitating. Ashamed that I had bought into the stereotyping of homosexuality that is so prevalent in the sports world.

But the worst was, I was the last one in the family to know—I should have been the first. I should have been there to stand beside him when he broke the news to the whole family. Sure, I was busy, but that's a poor excuse. First there was our own game against the Oregon State Beavers in the Insight Bowl, and then that night, the BCS championship game. I was completely focused on football. I wasn't there when he needed me the most.

Plus I had blamed Ravi because he was afraid to tell me—or at least it must have sounded like that to him. What I really meant to say was, what's wrong with me? Where was I when my little bro was working this out? And what kind of courage did it take for him to face me, the big brother, the campus jock, as well as the entire family?

Yeah, my feelings about this weren't simple, that's for sure. I felt horrible about some of my behavior, but I was so in awe of Ravi. And I also felt some fear. There are lots of places in this great land of ours where being different in any kind of way and not being quiet about it can make you a target. Ravi seems fearless. I admire that.

But still, I let him down. That day he stood taller than me, and not just because he's a half-inch taller. Okay, an inch. Whatever. He's a big guy, in every way that matters, and I look up to him.

And just so you know, about me letting him down, etc., Ravi would say I'm full of crap. Because he's that kind of brother.

GREAT COMPETITORS PLAY TO WIN

4

You show me a good loser and I'll show you a permanent one. — Y. Roth

LACKAWANNA TRAIL WAS OUR LOCAL HIGH SCHOOL, and Maya, Ravi and I had great experiences there. But for me, it was truly transforming, and all because of football.

For years, our Lackawanna Trail Lions were the little team with the giant heart, the team that would lose five games by an average of six points, the team that was always one play away from winning. As grade schoolers, Glenn, Woody, Vince and I would play our own game on the practice field while the varsity team fought it out on the main field. Then we'd plop down on the hill next to the scoreboard for the final quarter of the big guys matchup, where we'd watch our heroes come up just a bit short on third down on Friday night, or overthrow a bootleg pass by a few inches on Saturday afternoon. Then RB Mark Kaliwoski, WR Bobby Suprick (Jen's big brother), and QB Keith Schubert would walk off the field with their eyes to the ground— battered warriors covered in dirt, grass, and a little blood, with their fans cheering and clapping in the background. This was the ritual. Every week another loss, every week appreciative applause. I couldn't comprehend it.

Losing would crush the players, but the fans somehow accepted each defeat gracefully. With a strange mix of resignation and satisfaction, our team and our town embraced this coming-up-a-bit-short-while-exerting-great-effort mentality, and made it a way of life. Even at 8, I found this confusing.

And then when I was 10, after yet another Trail loss, Ravi and I watched an interview with Bobby Knight in which he was discussing winning and losing and the psychology behind each. Afterwards, when Ravi asked me what Coach Knight meant, it seemed simple: "You show me a good loser and I'll show you a permanent one." Once that thought hit me, I started to see a change in myself—an internal shift in what I believed I could accomplish.

Glenn, Woody, and Vince also adopted this phrase over the next few months, and together we refused to accept losing. And if there was one single moment when we knew we could never look back, it occurred three summers later. We were 13, and we were all playing in the local 3-on-3 basketball tournament in the city of Scranton. We'd already proven it to ourselves, but this was our chance to show all the city kids and Catholic League players that the kids from the sticks could play some ball.

We blazed through the tournament with only one loss, but ended up in the losers bracket of the playoffs. It was like starting all over again. To win the championship, we would not only have to win our way out, but also win two straight in the finals. No problem. We hustled our way through the losers bracket and brought ourselves to the finals, against the crowd favorites, the players from Scranton. We set the tone early, as Glenn elbowed one of their players to the ground—a foul we all enjoyed. Near the end of the game we were down 19-15, with the winner being the first team to reach 21 points. Then Woody took over and dropped three straight 2-point buckets from beyond the arc to send us into the final game against the same opponents. The winner would take home the title.

When we sat on the curb during our five-minute break we could see our opponents' anxious faces framed by a growing crowd. First 40 spectators, then 100, 200, then 300, finally 400! What? This was just a half-court game! As we broke our huddle, Vince looked each of us in the eye and said not a word. We were only 13, but we knew a win would change our little town forever. And we had no doubt we would win. Losing was no longer part of our vocabulary. The best part—we didn't avoid the pressure created by the crowd, our formidable opponents, or the high stakes. Instead, we invited it.

Again we began with a violent hit, this time a combined effort from Woody, Glenn and me as we blocked a sure lay-up. That trio on the other side of the court would have to sweat for every single point. March Madness had come to Scranton, and we'd brought it. With every point the local city boys scored, the crowd cheered; with every bucket we made, the crowd grew silent—well, until the spectators saw what was happening.

As we took the lead, the crowd began to turn. We out-played our opponents, mentally and physically, and proved to over 400 people watching a half-court 3-on-3 game on Scranton's Courthouse Square that we were in relentless pursuit of that competitive edge we had cultivated on the Dalton Courts. Silence became appreciation, jeers gave way to applause. By the end of the game, when we scored the final bucket, we didn't just deliver a shock to the basketball mindset in Scranton, we had a coming-out party of sorts for our own philosophy: compete to win, and never accept losing.

And the four of us, joined by many others at Lackawanna Trail, were just getting started. Our enthusiasm and positive attitude took a firm foothold in the Dalton sports world.

As athletes, our goal was to *always* outwork and out-compete our opponents. The fall of 1995, in week two of our high school football season, we brought that goal so close to us that we could touch it. It was a Saturday afternoon home game against Western Wayne in front of no more than 250 people. The Demon Deacons featured two all-conference rushers and a high-profile head coach. In typical Lackawanna Trail Lions fashion, we had a chance to win the game on the final drive.

We began on our own 30 with just over two minutes remaining and the score 14-6. Down the field we went.

> *Slant route for 15.*
> *Draw for 27.*
> *Hitch for 9.*
> *Slant for 10.*

I was a freshman, starting on varsity at wide receiver and cornerback. This game marked the start of what became known as the "R&R Connection"—I was getting open and QB Tim Ronchi was getting me the rock. Our team's confidence was growing with each snap. Before Western Wayne knew it, we were inside their ten-yard line.

It came down to 4th and goal from the 9-yard line with :07 on the clock. Two receivers on the left, and I was isolated to the right. Head Coach T. J. Fadden called a slant, Ronchi took a three-step drop, threw me a rope, and we executed. Touchdown Lions!

Still down two points with no time on the clock, we needed a two-point conversion to send the game into overtime. Otherwise, it would be the unthinkable: another Lions loss.

We called a run-off tackle to the right, and were stopped one yard from the Promised Land. The game ended with the football spotted three feet from the goal line, three feet from tying the score, three feet from breaking out of our Lackawanna Trail fatalistic attitude: great effort, but another loss.

As we walked into the locker room with our heads down, our senior leader began to speak to our team. "Good job, guys, don't hang your heads. We kept it close, we're getting better."

Okay, picture me, a 14-year-old freshman who didn't shave yet, was going through puberty, and, thanks to Glenn, used way too much LA Looks. And I was furious. Our leader, our *captain*, was telling us it is okay to lose.

I lost it.

God bless him, but I lost my mind on that guy with the loser mentality. My teammates watched and listened from a safer distance, but I got in his face.

"Okay to LOSE? Are you kidding me?"

Silence. Shock. I continued.

"We came CLOSE? Are you serious?"

I took a breath. I got even louder.

"This is not okay! Losing is never okay! 'Great effort' is for losers! Great competitors play to WIN!"

Yeah, it's a cliché to call it an out-of-body experience, but that's just how it felt. Even now, when I relive that moment in my mind, I'm knocked over by the passion, by the rage and intensity that gripped all of the newer players. I'm unsure if the message got through to the seniors, but us younger players had grown up expecting to win each time on the field, and our mentality was becoming contagious.

Although we finished that season 2-8, the other freshmen and sophomores on the varsity team understood: we didn't have to lose anymore.

Next season, with new coach Jeff Wasilchak and a new team, we finished 3-7, but we were turning the corner. The dark clouds hovering over our program for the past decade had begun to evaporate.

The following year, in 1998, the clouds were gone. Our competitive and winning mentality had spread throughout Lackawanna Trail to all its surrounding towns. A third of the way into the season, you would have thought someone struck gold under the Dalton Courts. Trail football signs were plastered everywhere. Local businesses were booming during the week and shutting down on Friday nights and Saturday afternoons for games, and attendance shot from 200 to 2,000 in a matter of weeks. For the first time ever, we were ranked in the top ten in football-crazy Pennsylvania.

Players had a blast. We were living the Pennsylvania lore of high school football and loving it with post-game parties and a homecoming dance after a victory. Of course, as with any successful high school football player, the girls we dated also got a little cuter. As we brought a community together over the sport of football, life was breathed into our little section of northeastern Pennsylvania.

And that was the year it finally happened: we won the conference championship. This brought us to the district final against the reigning state runner-up, the Riverside Vikings.

The district final was a game for the ages. The Veterans Memorial Stadium, home of the Vikings, was one of the most hostile places to play in PA—games there could draw ten thousand fans who, I swear, drank honey lemon ginger tea and spoke barely a word during the week in preparation for cheering and booing on that magnificent Friday evening.

Of course, we were the major underdogs and no one gave us a chance. It was a daunting personal challenge for me, too, as I would be covered by All-State defensive back Billy Kyttle and would myself be covering All-State wide receiver Eugene Gallagher. In my view, it couldn't have been scripted any better. We felt we were just as good as any team in America, and, personally, I felt I was better than both Kyttle and Gallagher. All we had needed was the stage on which to perform, in order to show the world we belonged. Now we had it.

We received first. The opening three plays of the game were passes from Ronchi to Roth as we led the team down the field. As the game went on, the battles intensified. Big play after big play, both teams remained aggressive. It was 21-14 Riverside at the half, and our team believed. The locker room was raucous to the point of being bone shattering. No coach needed to say a word, even if he could be heard over the noise. We knew we could play with them, we knew we could compete with them, we knew we could beat them.

But we didn't. The final score indicates a blowout, as Riverside ran all over us in the second half on their way to another appearance in the state playoffs. But the little Lions of Lackawanna Trail made their statement. Sure, we matched Riverside's intensity and proved we had great heart like past Trail teams, but this was different.

As the second-place medals were draped around our necks, I can remember feeling as if I were watching the ceremony from fifty yards away. I was stunned, bruised—and straight-up angry. I knew, our team knew, our whole town knew we were no longer going to accept losing. We were now a program, a mainstay in Pennsylvania high school football.

Why?

Because every member of that team clearly understood one thing: as Coach Bobby Knight taught Ravi and me years earlier, no one ever had to accept losing.

Good losers don't win, winners win.

During the next season, we had the awesome privilege of playing in what is considered one of the most dramatic and overall best high school football games in Pennsylvania history against the Dunmore Bucks. I had just come back from injuring my leg, and was thrilled to be a part of a night I'll never forget. Woody was even more excited. He'd gotten hurt during freshman and sophomore training camps, had taken his junior year off to focus on basketball, then returned for senior year training camp, where he was hurt again. All three times, it was due to some sort of collision with me, and he'd never let me forget it. When he scored the game-tying touchdown, though, all was forgiven. Glenn, meanwhile, set the Pennsylvania record for most yards thrown by a quarterback in a single quarter, and we were ranked as high as third in the state.

And that year we won the district final. Lackawanna Trail went on to win ten out of the next eleven district championships and developed a modern-day dynasty.

A mind-set was changed. A society was transformed. A mentality was ingrained.

And all because of high school football. Who would have thought?

I'm Gonna Be a Panther

5

THERE'S A BLUEPRINT FOR THE FIRST YEAR OF COLLEGE. Arrive in the fall, party a little too much, cheat on the high school girlfriend, get dumped by the high school girlfriend, get drunk and call the high school girlfriend, and then pass out with the girl down the hall who has just cheated on her high school boyfriend…with you. You lose touch with the people you said you would never forget, and, finally, by second semester, you're talking to only two or three friends from childhood.

Amazingly, though, you also get closer with your parents. They become easier to talk to, you actually want to talk to them, and, for some reason, you think it's cool to call them at 1:00 AM, borderline blackout, and say "I love you guys" as O.A.R.'s Crazy Game of Poker is being blasted in your boy Jim's SAE frat house (go ahead, admit it).

I was looking forward to all of this—but mostly I was counting down the days until college football. My school of choice was the University of Pittsburgh, otherwise known as Pitt, and I chose to walk on to the football team as a wide receiver. Walking on meant no guaranteed scholarship, but I was willing to take that chance. I had also looked at Ithaca College, a smaller school where I'd be guaranteed playing time, and Delaware, a D-I AA program where football was the center of attention and, coincidentally, where my high school girlfriend would be taking classes and cheerleading. Deep down, though, I knew I had to play Division I football, and I had to go to Pitt.

Well, not exactly. Growing up in Dalton you cheered for one of two college football teams: Penn State or Notre Dame. Since Glenn and Woody were Penn State fans and Vince was the lone Notre Dame fan, my allegiance went to the Fighting Irish just to even things up. Each Saturday from 3rd grade on, I would turn on NBC or whatever channel Notre Dame was on, put on my oversized ND fitted hat, and cheer like crazy. From Lou Holtz and Tony Rice to local northeastern Pennsylvania heroes Raghib 'The Rocket' Ismail and Ron Powlus, whose signed football and picture would adorn my bedroom wall, my football heroes wore the Blue and Gold. Plus, Lackawanna Trail alum George Hayduk, who worked the p.a. system at all the high school games, had been a defensive lineman there. As if that weren't enough, Notre Dame had been the final stop that Dad, Ravi and I had made on our summer college tour around the nation. So, my future was set: I would play for Notre Dame and make plays in the Golden Dome.

Unfortunately their coaching staff did not agree with my life plans. But like the beautiful girl who smiles at you during class and seems intrigued, so were the Irish. So, after my junior year at Lackawanna Trail, I went to their summer camp, where I learned that they would offer only one scholarship to a wide receiver. And I was told it was going to Ronnie Rodamer, a 6'5" 215 lb. freak of an athlete from West Virginia. One of the most coveted players in the nation, he was projected as a young Randy Moss—but I still felt I was better. The Irish coaches made sure Ronnie was first in line for each drill, but I made sure I was right there in his hip pocket, challenging myself and even trying to make him prove he was better than me on every snap. I'm sure he never considered me a threat to his scholarship offer, but in my eyes the competition was on.

By the end of the camp, I felt confident that I could play Division I football and that I could play it at Notre Dame. The Irish, however, were not swayed by my self-assurance, and failed to come up with an offer. A few months after that I e-mailed a recruiting guru, and asked him why Notre Dame and other Division I schools were not making a scholarship offer to me when I felt I had performed as well as or even outperformed my counterparts the previous summer. His response: "Yogi—you're a good player, but it's not fair to yourself to compare your ability to that of Ronnie Rodamer. I would look at smaller schools. You're not a Division I talent." When I read

Mr. Guru's e-mail, I made my decision with relative ease: I was going to play at the highest level—period.

So... near the end of my senior season at Lackawanna Trail, I was on my way to visit Pitt, the lone Division I school who continued to recruit me. I'd been to their summer camps three years in a row and won MVP the previous June. The offensive coordinator and wide receiver's coach, J. D. Brookhart, was a guy who had influenced me from the moment we met. As we continued our relationship, I would learn that he too was lightly recruited, had his size and speed questioned, and eventually walked on to Colorado State. He left that university as its sixth all-time leading receiver.

On my visit, the Panthers happened to be playing in their last appearance in Pitt Stadium, it happened to be against Notre Dame, and I just happened to have three tickets. So I invited Vince to hop into the car with my dad and me and join in the fun.

We were there for one of the most historic games in Pitt football history—on November 13, 1999, they beat the Fighting Irish on the final drive of the game, winning 31-27. As the clock struck :00, the fans poured onto the field, ripping up strips of turf in a wild frenzy. Then they took the goalposts and ran them down Forbes Avenue, and I sat there, checking out the scene, and felt as much in my element as I had ever felt. Total chaos reigned everywhere, but in the midst of it, I was quite comfortable. It was football at its finest and I knew Pitt would be my home for the next four years. But it had nothing to do with their communications program or their dorms. None of that mattered at this point. The only thing that I cared about was that this university shared in my growing desire to beat those who said no to me, who almost dared me to prove them wrong, and the University of Notre Dame and Ronnie Rodamer would be on our schedule for three of the next four seasons. That in itself was enough.

I was going to be a Panther, and was never more proud of my decision.

LOCKER 106

6

THE BIG DAY HAD FINALLY ARRIVED. And really, it was probably quite typical of the many scenes being played out on college campuses all over the country. There in front of Sutherland Hall stood the emotional mom, the proud dad, the eager son. I'm sure my father had words of wisdom (he always did), and I'm sure my mother sniffled and carried on, and I'm sure I listened carefully, and reassured them all would be well.

Not even close. I remember nothing except my dad's lips were moving, my mom's eyes were blinking, and all I could think of was, "It's ball time. Let's go. Let's do this." I was extremely focused, and I was ready to show how my off-season preparation had increased my ability. I was primed to prove that I was Division I football talent.

The previous spring Dad and I had driven the five hours to Pittsburgh so that I could check out practice a couple of times. I'd call Coach Brookhart and Coach Tom Freeman, asking for film, playbooks, training manuals, whatever they had. Then in June and July I attended a couple of weeklong off-season workouts. I'd familiarized myself with the pace of Division I football, and I'd met some players. The receiving corps, led by Latef Grim, Antonio Bryant, R. J. English, Lamar Slade, Chris Curd, and Tim Stein took me in and seemed to enjoy having me around, despite what I'm told was an excess of questions on my part. I knew, though, that I needed every advantage I could get, and that I couldn't waste a moment. I wasn't a scholarship player, but I felt I was good enough to be one, and if anyone could give me the chance to prove that, it was Coach Brookhart. Whatever the players could tell me, I would put to good use.

And, at last, here it was—my first day in training camp. Me, a Division I wide receiver. I entered the locker room excited but not in awe, prepared but not uptight, driven but not rattled. And then I couldn't find my locker.

Round and round I looked. Nothing. First the lockers near the tens, then the twenties, all the way up to the eighties. Still nothing. After a while the equipment man named "Ox" lumbered into view, wiped sweat from his eyes, and called out, "Hey Roth, you lookin' for your locker?"

"Um, yeah…" I said, pathetically trying to conceal my embarrassment.

"It's over there, back in the corner."

"In the corner?" I said to myself. Mind you, I never knew this particular corner of the locker room even existed, let alone would be my humble abode for the next few years.

I headed over to my spot. Ox was right, it was indeed in the corner. In a wooden lock-box marked with my name, sandwiched between another locker and the wall, I found my mesh bag, jersey, oversized Adidas high-top spikes, a helmet with a defensive lineman's facemask, and a pair of cotton shorts with five pockets. I later learned that this was what was formally called a 'girdle.'

After my initial shock at not having a real locker, and of sharing my jersey number with two other players, I realized that this was the only way I wanted it to be—hard.

Locker 106 became my home, and I couldn't have been more motivated. I immediately set my new goal: to move out of the corner and into the 'real' locker room, where, I was told, the 'real' players were.

Thanks, though, to the spring practice visits and the summer workouts, I actually felt at ease, and like I belonged. Heading into rookie camp, two days of freshmen-only practice, I felt 100% prepared. Cool, confident, poised— that was me. Ready for the big introductory meeting. Then all of a sudden I couldn't remember if we were supposed to have our pads on, whether we should bring our gear to the meeting, or even where to find the wide receiver meeting room in this brand-new facility.

So I showed up a minute late. Coach Brookhart hit me square between the eyes with his cold stare, reminiscent of my dad's when I'd screwed up. "You're late. We do not show up late here." He then began his opening speech, which centered on accountability. Sweet.

"Great job, Yogi," I said to myself.

It felt like our meeting was a week long and I sweated through an entire shirt before ever running a single route as a Panther. By the end, I was wondering if the coaches at Ithaca or Delaware would still take my call.

After two days of rookie camp, I knew I'd played well, felt confident, but could really sense the distance between Pittsburgh and Dalton. That night before our first practice with our entire roster, as I lay in my bed in my dorm, it hit me all at once. Poignant would be the diplomatic way to describe it; pitiful was more like it. I was not crying, I promise. Dust got in my eye. "I miss my girl... I miss my family... Locker 106—what the...? This is not what I signed up for... Just give me a chance... Is tomorrow gonna be worse?" I pictured Ox once again shooing me over to my dismal little corner, and I stared at the ceiling, wondering what the heck was I doing here.

Surprisingly, the world did not stop, and the 2000 Pitt Panthers did practice the next morning. On my walk to the field, I made up my mind that none of that stuff bothering me the night before would affect me now, because out there it was 11-on-11. Nothing more, nothing less. No one cared what number you wore, what locker you had, or what accolades you'd won. We only cared about competing. I had to trust that thought—I had no choice. And I was either going to compete or find myself on a Greyhound back to Dalton.

We started with a blocking drill; I was the scout team defender. Our strongest and, as I learned quickly, most unpredictable player, R. J., was about to block me. I shed his block and made the tackle, and he, all 6'4" and 220 pounds of him, grabbed me by the throat, and snarled something to the effect of "Don't be a hero." Yeah, I wondered how fast he could kill me with his bare hands, but I would not let him intimidate me. It's simple: as a freshman, there's a moment where you have to step up. For me, it was now. I stepped up with a shove, some trash talking, and another shove.

True, I didn't move him much, probably not even an inch, but I sent a message that I knew only one way to play, and that I was not going to back down to him or anyone else. I didn't send that message to R.J. necessarily; I sent it to myself.

As we dragged ourselves back to the dorms that night, R. J. came up to me and said, "Sorry, man, I get a little crazy out there. Good stuff. I like your style."

Hmmm. Style. The kid from Dalton in locker 106 got himself some style. Yeah.

TRAVEL SQUAD

7

"Humility comes before honor." – Proverbs 18:12

GAME WEEK ARRIVED BEFORE WE KNEW IT. I'd survived, and was the third flanker on the depth chart. But an even more important goal had yet to be met: making the travel squad. This was way cooler than not making the travel squad. You'd get to stay in a fancy hotel the night before the game, whether it was at home or away, you'd be there for the Friday night meeting in the hotel, and you'd get the cool warm-up suit.

Travel squad was by no means a sure thing for me. Yeah, I'd been pretty good in high school—All-State twice, and then Pennsylvania Defensive Player of the Year when I was a senior. But this was college football, Division I football, a whole new level for me. And Pitt, with a number of gifted players, was poised to have one of its most competitive seasons in years.

I'd learn my fate not by having a dramatic face-to-face meeting with Coach Brookhart or Head Coach Walt Harris, but instead by simply checking the list posted after practice Thursday on the team bulletin board in the locker room. Not enough suspense for me, apparently, because I made a slow approach, then cruelly noted every detail: the silver thumbtack, the brown corkboard, the white list headed by the title "Kent State Travel Roster." It was alphabetical, and I started at the top, making my way down the page, slowly, line by line. If eyes can move at a snail's pace, mine did.

Bryant, Carroll...

Gibboney, Grim...

Lee, Levy...

Pietricello, Roth, Rutherford....

I did a double take.

Pietricello, **Roth**, Rutherford....

Yes, it says Roth! I made it!

That night I couldn't wait to call home to give the family the news. I tried several times—the phone rang and rang, but no one answered, which was odd. Finally, Mom called back.

"Hey, did you make it?" she asked.

"Yeah, I did."

"Congratulations! We're so proud of you," she said, just a bit too quickly.

Something was up, I could tell by her tone. "Mom, what is it? What's wrong?"

"Yogi, your brother was in an accident today on the way to school. It was bad." She was unnaturally calm about this, especially for someone who can tend toward the dramatic, so I knew it was probably worse than bad.

Ravi was on his way to school, she told me, when he and his friends made the left onto the road that went to the high school. They were struck by an oncoming car, T-boned. Riding in the front passenger seat, Ravi took the brunt of the impact. His right femur was shattered in 17 places, his left tibia and fibula utterly destroyed.

I had to pry more details out of her, and it just kept getting worse and worse. He'd been knocked out immediately, which I guess was a blessing, but was losing body fluids rapidly as the rescuers worked frantically to extricate him. By then, Mom had arrived, and watched as the Jaws of Life pulled him out of what she described as looking like "a big crushed Coke can." He was in surgery through the night; a rod was placed in his right leg, and multiple screws in the left. Glenn, Woody, and Vince had called my parents as soon as they heard, as if he were their own little brother. Which in a way, he was.

Ravi soon rolled out of the hospital in good spirits, despite the agonizing pain from his injuries, and set himself a goal: he'd be on his feet to perform in the high school play a short four months away. Silently, we all hoped he'd be able to walk normally again, no matter when.

Every parent will tell you, the absolute worst thing to witness is pain to your children. You wish you could take that pain away and put it into your own body, just to make your child's suffering stop, and you dream of miracles. But my parents immediately rose past that—sure, they comforted Ravi, but they also propelled him toward recovery. No whining, no complaining, no excuses. They were tough—and they constantly reminded Ravi of the goal he had set. Every night our friend and local physical therapist, Mark Lombardi, would push Ravi through a set of exercises that were neither easy nor comfortable. Mom and Dad remained optimistic, and Ravi recovered the old-fashioned way, through hard work and a positive mental outlook. Quite simply, he humbly accepted the task before him—he knew he faced a monumental challenge before he could once again hear applause ringing in his ears.

While Ravi was rebuilding his mangled body, which had to have been torment, I was completely occupied by football. This freshman season was all-important: I had to separate myself from the pack and prove I was not just a practice player, not just another body, but that I was worthy of seeing the field.

Game one that year was a home game against Kent State, and my name was on that all-important travel roster. Warm-ups came and it felt just like Lackawanna Trail. I was catching passes, running routes, and preparing to play—in my first game as a Division I college player. This would be one for the books, I hoped. All I can tell you now is that we had plenty of weather there in Pittsburgh, including lightning, which forced a couple of game delays. No lightning struck me, though: I stayed on the bench throughout the game but was thrilled to be there as we ripped through the Golden Flashes 30-7.

Our second game held out more promise. This time an away game, we'd meet Bowling Green in our first nationally televised contest. ESPN2 would cover it, and I knew the world would be watching, or at least the world of Dalton. Then Coach Brookhart pulled me aside before practice on Thursday and told me there might not be room for me.

"Yogi, the numbers just aren't working out. It looks like we're not going to be able to take you."

I had to think fast.

"Coach, my parents already booked their flight. Should I have them cancel it?"

Coach gave me that look I'm sure he reserved for the most high-maintenance freshman, then he blinked, looked away, and looked back at me without saying a word. Then he shook his head "no" and growled, "Let me see what we can do. Hang on."

Now I knew for a fact that my parents were not flying to the middle of Ohio. World travelers though they may have been, I don't think they'd really ever heard of Bowling Green or Doyt L. Perry Stadium. And they certainly had no intention of going to a game there just as Ravi was getting out of the hospital after a near-fatal car accident. But my goal for that first season was to get on the travel team and stay there. So I extended the domain of truth into the realm of reasonable possibility, or, in plain English, I lied.

After practice I went back to the bulletin board, and there, for the second consecutive week, it read "Pietricello, Roth, Rutherford." And I didn't feel bad about it.

We'd overnight in a hotel before the game, and our director of football operations, Chris LaSala, figured I'd be the perfect roommate for Antonio Bryant. A.B. was easily our best player; he was also easily our loudest and our most volatile. Other than that, we were almost identical—he was from the rough section of downtown Miami, and I was from the rough section of downtown Dalton. Except that Dalton barely has a downtown, or even a section, much less a rough section. This would be interesting.

For five hours that night A.B. and I talked about life, the high school girlfriends we were still dating, family, Pitt, and the NFL. We dissected religion, poverty and politics; we discussed dedication, competitiveness, and the upcoming game. For five hours A.B. and I connected on a level that many friends never reach. That was the beauty of it—you'd think there would be issues between us, but there weren't. He was able to get who I was, and I was able to understand A.B., his approach to the game, and how similar we were at heart.

A.B. was a competitor through and through. If you didn't want to win as badly as he did, then he was going to leave you behind. And he was not afraid to let you know about it. Maybe some guys found him a little intense, a little obsessed, and were threatened by that. To me it felt normal, appropriate—and yeah, a little loud. And I liked it.

At the end of the night, he asked me what I wanted in life. I told him all I ever wanted was a chance to compete. And he said, "Yogi, tomorrow I'm going to show the world who I am, and tomorrow, you are going to play. You'll get your chance. That's a promise."

I didn't hear the alarm the next morning. It was drowned out by Bone Thugs-n-Harmony, with a little gospel thrown in—A.B. was ironing his clothes and getting into his zone. Although it was way too loud for my 6:00 a.m. taste, and borderline damaging to A.B.'s eardrums, the kid from locker 106 who just finessed his coach into keeping him on the travel roster wasn't about to complain.

Noon kickoff came around, and there I was, with the four other freshmen who had traveled, following around Coach Harris like little pests, just trying to get on national television. A.B. was ripping from the onset. First TD was a 56-yard bomb on a post. After he scored, he raced over to me, grabbed my facemask, and said, "Yogi, that was for you."

Second TD was a 29-yarder on a corner route. After he reached the end zone, he rushed over to me, grabbed me by the facemask, and again said, "Yogi, that was for you."

His third and final TD was a 47-yarder on a streak. Now, I was going ballistic on the sideline because a) I knew I must be getting on tv since A.B. and I were celebrating after each touchdown, and b) I thought that I had a real chance to get in. Sure enough, A.B. came over to me after his third score, grabbed me by the facemask, and said, "I told you I'd get you in!"

So it was 34-3 toward the end of the third quarter, and I was watching A.B. on the phone talking to Coach Brookhart, who was upstairs in the booth. I could see A.B. pleading with him. Ox (ironic, yes?) then called me over to the phone. "Coach Brook wants you."

"Hello...? Hello...? Hello...?"

No answer. I couldn't hear anything.

Then I realized that my helmet was still on. I ripped it off, and calmly and coolly said, "Hey, Coach," except that it came out in this dorky multi-pitched croak that I thought I'd left behind with puberty.

"Yogi, we want to red-shirt you, so I don't think you're going to play," Coach Brookhart told me.

I didn't pause for a second. "Okay, Coach," I shot back, "but only red-shirt me if you can guarantee me a scholarship right now." Wondering what I just said to the guy who only weeks earlier was ripping me for being late to his first meeting, I awaited a reply.

He seemed a little taken aback, but responded, "Yogi, I think you'll get one, but I can't guarantee it right now. It's the end of the 3rd quarter!"

"Okay, then put me in because I'm only going to pay for four years of school."

And there you have it. Wearing #31, my third jersey of the year, two games into the season, I was on the field, and on ESPN2. The first play was a run to my side. Elated and euphoric, I threw a nice, clean block to the throat of the DB I was up against. The boys were yelling from the sideline, and my life couldn't have gotten any better—I was playing Division I football! To make it even sweeter, we cruised past Bowling Green 34-16.

Who knows why A.B. and I were roommates that night, or why we connected so well. But from that point on, my confidence grew, my playing time increased, and, yes, I moved out of the corner and into a new locker (but kept the same nameplate). While A.B. did get me on the field as a freshman and was my travel roommate for two years after that, he also taught me a lesson that stays with me to this day.

"Yogi," A.B. said to me that night in Ohio, "never forget that humility comes before honor."

Frankly, I didn't really understand what he meant, or why he was so intent on making me grasp that thought. Maybe he was talking about himself. He'd had a nerve-wracking path to Pitt the previous year before becoming their final scholarship player, and now, this year, he was hitting his stride. But maybe it was about me—locker 106 was certainly a humble beginning, and I'd now made it onto the field in our second game as a walk-on from Dalton.

Or maybe it was meant to hit closer to home. Back in August, as I met my objective of making the travel squad, my little brother had found his newest and most difficult challenge lay directly ahead of him. I wish I could say Ravi leaned on me during his long recovery, but the opposite is more like it. I was pulling inspiration from him, as he wheeled himself around the Carrier Dome while I rode the pine at Syracuse. And when I started as a freshman on special teams during the West Virginia game on Thanksgiving Day, he was there to cheer me on. His remarkable and hard-fought return to strength was head and shoulders above my hunger for travel squad status, I knew that.

Finally, true triumph came for Ravi on December 5, when he starred as Professor Van Helsing in *Dracula*, exactly 101 days after his accident.

Humility comes before honor. First, understand who you are, and where you are—and then cut loose, go for it, let it rip. Don't hold back.

THE PHONE CALL

8

SOPHOMORE YEAR STARTED WITH A BANG. We were break-
ing in a new stadium, Heinz Field, in downtown Pittsburgh, and were coming off of our most successful season in 11 years. Excitement filled the air as
we returned a variety of starters and set our sights on making ourselves serious contenders on the college football scene. We opened the season against
a Division I-AA team, East Tennessee State. Not much of an opponent on
paper, but it didn't matter. We had something to prove and that night, in a
packed stadium, we were going to do it.

Early in the game we forced East Tennessee to punt, and A.B. returned
it close to the end zone. But as he was tackled, he sprained his ankle. In an
instant, I was on the field in the first quarter, playing Division I football
when the game mattered. This was a big deal to my parents and friends in
the stands, but for me, it was just the expected outcome of all my hard work.
I ended up playing well, and even almost scored, catching 5 passes, returning
a few punts, converting a few key third downs, and absolutely loving playing
at this level. It felt normal, it felt right, it felt… well, incredible. We blew out
East Tennessee 31-0.

We celebrated into the night on Pitt's campus and I began to feel what
it was like to be a Division I football player off the field. Random guys were
congratulating me and random girls were smiling at me. One of the head
cheerleaders came up to me that night at a party and said, "You're a football

player, everyone heard your name tonight… life is only going to get better. Every girl here knows who you are." Life was indeed pretty good.

But fame is fleeting, which I already knew. My dad would remind me after games in high school, "What have you done for me lately, son?" with a smile that meant I had to keep working, keep competing. It was no surprise to me that I would have to prove myself all over again the next week. And South Florida was a formidable opponent. The Bulls had a roster full of Miami, Florida and Florida State transfers and were much more athletic than we were. That talent, along with a swagger they'd borrowed from the University of Miami and a 100-degree temperature that afternoon at Heinz Field, combined to make for a very unfortunate day. We lost a game that was dubbed "the worst loss in Pitt history" and I was in the starting line-up.

Add to that misery, I was hit so hard after a catch that I couldn't walk for two days, and my Mom went from jubilation a week earlier to seeing the next day's Pittsburgh paper which read something to the effect of "Not only is it bad that Pitt lost, but they lost with some kid named Yogi Zohar Roth starting at wide receiver." In seven days I went from being the man to not wanting to show my face outside my dorm.

We were sent reeling from that loss, and then got overwhelmed in short order by Miami, Notre Dame, and Syracuse. The staff feared for their jobs, the players were miserable as we watched our dreams of bowl contention fade, and most of us just wanted the season to end.

But then came our trip to Boston College. We took a 7-0 lead, but watched it vanish as we were blown out 45-7. The Panthers were in an absolute tailspin—and after the game our team got an earful from Coach Harris. In as passionate a speech as I had ever seen him give, this cerebral offensive wizard came out of his skin. He called out every player, coach, trainer and even manager. The crux of what he said was simple: if you want to turn this around, show up on Monday. If not, stay home. Because we *will* turn this around.

What occurred over the next two months was nothing short of miraculous. We knocked off Virginia Tech, who had been ranked #5 in the nation the previous week, and just like that, had our confidence back. We roared through the rest of our season and faced off against North Carolina State in the Tangerine Bowl. Like we had done the previous five games, we physically dominated the Wolfpack en route to a 34-19 victory. Six straight wins had capped our amazing turnaround, and it could have been argued that we were the hottest team in the entire nation. I had played a lot, was important to the squad, and had the sense that my goal of a scholarship was right around the corner.

Early in the off-season I was called into Coach Harris's office. We sat down and chatted about the culture of the team, the young receivers, and how Rod Rutherford, our new quarterback, was doing. Coach Harris and I had a unique relationship for a coach and his player—we actually talked man to man, not just coach to player. I certainly had a high opinion of him as our head coach, and he in turn respected my work ethic. Still, though, I had no scholarship.

By now these talks were somewhat of a ritual. I met with him after my freshman season, freshman spring practice, and now, after my sophomore season, to ask him what I needed to do to see more playing time. And most importantly, where I stood regarding a scholarship. I felt I had earned the right to ask him, and he was always honest. So, while I disagreed with his decisions during our previous two meetings, I felt this might be the day. And it was.

"Yogi, we're putting you on full scholarship. Congratulations, you've earned it."

Two long years of struggle, over, just like that. No, I didn't leap up out of that fancy chair in his office and jump for joy. Instead, I just smiled, said thank you, gave him a hug and walked straight to Coach Brookhart's office.

Coach Brookhart was the guy who had stood by me, inserted me into the line-up, and, I would learn later, even saw a little of himself in me. I felt I owed him everything, and loved him because he had stood on the so-called 'table' for me so many times, not only as my position coach, but as my mentor and friend. After getting congrats from him and two other special mentors, offensive line Coach Tom Freeman (who had recruited me from Dalton) and Chris LaSala, I walked down the long hallway of our facility, down the stairway to the locker room where the guys from our receiving corps were waiting for me. They knew of these annual meetings with Coach Harris, and they were all pulling for me.

I walked in and Lamar Slade was the first person I saw. We smiled, he started to jump around, and all of the wide receivers celebrated. By the end, the other players would join in and I was officially out of the corner and locker 106, and into locker 82. But I wouldn't forget where I came from: I brought over the locker 106 nameplate, complete with the taped-on #82 that some players had put up when I had gotten my legit receiver's number that fall. As great as all that was, though, I had an important call to make.

I waited until dusk and I was walking alone through the streets of Squirrel Hill, on my way to share the news with Michele Rosenthal, who had become one of my closest friends and mentors while interning for her in the Pittsburgh mayor's office. I stopped, pulled out my red Nokia mobile phone and dialed.

"Hello."

"Hey Mom, is Dad there?"

"Yeah, why? What's the matter? Is everything alright?"

I knew this would be her response—it was always the same whenever I asked for Dad.

"Yeah, I just need to talk to both of you."

She called for Dad to pick up the other line from the garage, where he was working on his motorcycle, and I began to get the chills. This was the moment I had dreamt of. I was over getting a scholarship to validate my Division I football player status; I knew I'd proven myself against Bowling Green, East Tennessee State, North Carolina State, and others. I didn't need to see my name in the paper; it already appeared there to commemorate my involvement in the South Florida catastrophe. I didn't need a cheerleader to tell me I was cool; I was dating a great gal.

I wanted to earn that scholarship so I could call my parents. I wanted to tell my dad in particular that he didn't have to write another check for the rest of his life on my behalf. That our hard work had paid off. That for the first time in my life, I could give them something back.

As I told them the news, I could hear their voices fill with pride as they congratulated me. Then Dad asked me, "Yogi, would you have rather been offered a scholarship straight out of high school, or earn it this way?"

I didn't have to answer—we all knew what I would say.

"Son, life is about the journey—don't forget that. We're proud of you."

We hung up. I got the chills again. Then I worked out.

THE 29-YARD LINE

9

WITH THOSE WORDS "FULL SCHOLARSHIP" ringing in my ears, I headed into the next year poised to have a stellar junior season. I'd ended spring practice near the top of the depth chart, and was physically stronger and mentally more prepared than I had ever been.

I spent the off-season working out from 6 a.m. to 11 a.m., then interning at the mayor's office from noon to 5. I capped it off with evenings at the new bar in Pittsburgh called High-Tops. No, not drinking—I was the bouncer, all 5' 11" of me. I'd also get in extra workouts after cleaning up the bar at 3 a.m., courtesy of Duquesne University, whose security lights lit their turf field 24 hours a day. I needed an edge, and was finding it in those extra workouts and weekend throwing sessions with Rod Rutherford, our starting quarterback. Plus, A.B. had left college early to enter the NFL draft, so I figured I'd have a good chance to become a starter in the fall.

Fall camp began, though, and two recruits began to play better and better each day. One would not only beat me out after one game, but would become a sophomore All-American, Biletnikoff Award winner, and Heisman Trophy finalist. That's right, I competed for playing time with Larry Fitzgerald, widely considered one of the best receivers in the history of college ball. Now he's a Pro Bowler and a household name after being chosen by the Arizona Cardinals as the third overall pick in the 2004 NFL draft. He was also the best travel roommate I ever had—for one thing, he wasn't bumping Bone

Thugs-n-Harmony first thing every morning.

While Larry and I had a lot of laughs as Panthers and continue to do so with monthly updates on football, traveling and our personal lives, the receiver who made the most lasting impact on me beyond the field was another guy entirely. It was Billy Gaines, a 5' 7" white kid from Ijamsville, Maryland.

Coach Brookhart had met a small, explosive receiver during Pitt's high school summer camp the previous year, and had described him to me as "tough, relentless, with great hands." And he was fast. Coach probably said that a couple of times. While any player with this skill set was an obvious bonus for the team, it was also another competing player at the position I wanted. But who knows why, this kid out of Maryland grew on me—and we had yet to meet.

That December, Coach Brookhart called me up and asked me to host Billy on his official visit. The host got about $30 bucks and a free dinner, so I quickly agreed. From the moment Billy walked into the Hampton Inn on campus sporting a grey hooded sweatshirt, I knew I liked him. There were no pretensions about him at all—he wasn't dressed up, wasn't there to impress anyone, he was simply Billy, or from that point on, B.G.

We went back to my apartment in the heart of campus and did what most college kids did—played video games. I wasn't much of a gamer, like my two roommates Andy Lee and J.B. Gibboney were, but I could hold my own.

The game served only as a backdrop for our conversation. We talked about being undersized white receivers who had chips on our shoulders, but mostly we vented about how much we hated being compared to Rudy Ruetigger. Not because Rudy didn't have a great story, but because, B.G. and I would say in unison, "He wasn't even a good player!"

He and I struck a bond that weekend and stayed in touch throughout the off-season. He would drive his beat-up pick-up truck to Pitt for spring practice, would constantly question me about the offense, and was one of the first to congratulate me on receiving a scholarship. It was a great relationship because although I knew we would be competing for the same position, I actually welcomed it, because our similar mind-sets brought out the best in each other.

That season, Billy's first and my third, was a long one: I began it by getting injured, while Billy ended it by breaking a bone in his foot. He played a decent amount, but like most first-year players, had difficulty adjusting to the college game, to say nothing of balancing sports and academics. Like the sheer competitor he was, though, B.G. quickly found his path. After a few games, he was playing well, learning the offense, and still finding time for his classes and his girlfriend, Natalie.

Near the end of the season came that game at Miami, the one that denied us a share of the conference crown. B.G. didn't travel because his injury had ended his season, so he was watching at home. As that game went on and we attempted to break their 31-game winning streak, I finally got on the field, only to have us lose on the final play as a ball sailed past my outstretched arms. Of course I had wanted to catch the ball to win the game, but I also wanted to prove that smaller guys like B.G. and I could make the big play. I can truthfully say I was devastated after that play, and that game. I called home, then dragged myself to the team bus, half-heartedly checking text messages. Then one struck me: "Proud of you, Yog, so proud of you. Thanks for everything—B.G."

After a disappointing loss to West Virginia, our season ended with us dominating Oregon State to capture a bowl victory—our second in two years and our first back-to-back bowl victories in over twenty years. Still, it wasn't the ending we'd hoped for, but it was something to build on.

 So I turned my attention to preparing for my final year at Pitt, and B.G. began his rehab. It was a long road for him, and though he was getting healthier, he knew he wasn't playing up to his potential. We'd often find ourselves sitting outside of study hall at the sandwich shop, Billy in that same grey hoodie he'd worn the first time we met, and we'd talk about life and football, and how to get through it all. During spring practice he gained confidence, but he also began to consider transferring colleges or changing positions. His passion for the game was fading; I could see this on the practice field and in the weight room. Simply put, Billy had lost his swagger.

Every college football player goes through this funk. You lose confidence, you think of other options, and you forget how much fun the game of football is. Trust me, I could relate.

So, that summer, after each workout, B. G. and I began to stay after practice. We'd throw the ball, laugh, talk route running, secondary coverages, linebacker recognition and how the upcoming season would be a blast. Day after day, I'd ask him, "Hey B.G., did you have fun today?" And day after day, he'd look at me, smoothly catch my passes, smirk and say, "Nope, not yet." It became a funny little ritual, but with each day, each workout, each throw, and each conversation B.G. would have a little more fun and put a little more passion into his game.

It was a Tuesday, June 17, when I finally got the answer I'd been waiting for. I can remember we were just leaving our indoor facility on Pittsburgh's South Side when I asked him, "Did you have fun today?" He took a sec, then said, in his laid-back way, "You know what—today I had a blast. Football was fun again."

Now that was the B.G. I knew, the B.G. who led his high school team to four straight state championships and 50 straight wins. It was the B.G. who had the ability to start on our team, score touchdowns, become a fan favorite and someday perhaps even watch his #29 jersey sell out from the campus bookstore. After our throwing session we went inside to the weight room to go through Coach Dave Kennedy's strength and conditioning workout. I watched B.G., who had always been an absolute stud in the weight room, fly through his workout with a glow about him that had been missing for these many long months. Coach Kennedy picked up on it right away, and hollered, "Who is this guy? Is this the Billy Gaines that we know? Is the masked man back?" We all could see it—B.G. had his swagger once again. He was back on his feet.

As he strode out of the weight room in his cut-off Pitt t-shirt, I called out to him, "Yo, B.G., you have fun today!" This time it wasn't a question. And #29 looked back over his right shoulder, gave his trademark half-smile and half-smirk, and declared, "Yeah, man, I'm back!"

That night B.G. and a few of the guys had a cookout at the church where Billy was staying. His old apartment had burned down a few weeks before—an electrical problem had started a fire in his bedroom shortly after he woke up from a nap. Billy ran back up to his room five minutes later to find his bed in flames. So the former convent next door was now Billy's temporary home, along with a few other players who'd also had to evacuate. You might say Billy had a lot to be thankful for—he'd survived the fire, and had just rekindled his love for football that very morning. But what had begun as a night of celebration and new beginnings turned into a night we would all love to go back and change.

Around 2:30 in the morning, Billy and his friends went onto the roof to overlook the Pittsburgh skyline, have a few laughs, and begin to wind down the evening. On their way back into the church, Billy decided to explore. He noticed a door he had seen days earlier and he and a teammate climbed through it, into a small crawlspace above the ceiling of the church, all 2x4's and thin sheetrock. As he crawled deeper and deeper into the space, it got darker and darker, until finally he realized it was time to turn around. Yet when he began to crawl back, he must have put his weight on something other than the makeshift catwalk, and in that instant, B.G. lost his footing.

Thirty feet straight down he dropped, hitting his head on a pew. His teammates rushed to his side, called 911, gave him CPR, and prayed that he would regain consciousness. The paramedics arrived and Billy still had a pulse. Miraculously, he was still with us.

Word spread quickly, and early the next morning I rushed into Coach Brookhart's office, where he assured me, "It's serious, but he should be okay." I breathed a sigh of relief and went into the empty team meeting room and sat down next to Larry. Five minutes later, Coach Brookhart stuck his head in the door and said, "It doesn't look good—we should get to the hospital."

"Doesn't look good" didn't register as "might not make it." I mean, how could it? We were Division I athletes, we were invincible. Within hours the whole team had gathered at Mercy Hospital. When we walked in, Billy's entire town was already there, old teammates, family friends, even his priest. They told us that his hometown was hosting a vigil on Billy's old football field, praying for his recovery. His impact and influence in that room was so strong you could touch it, and it was comforting to know that so many teammates from so many squads were pulling for him. The silences were horrible and awkward, but seeing his parents and his younger brothers Michael and Nick was what could rip your heart out. When we hugged in that cold sterile hallway of Mercy was when I first felt that B.G. might not live another day.

Amazingly, there were no broken bones, we found out, but Billy had suffered severe brain damage from the fall. After a few hours, we were allowed to see him. I waited and was one of the last people to walk into Billy's room. I think part of it was that I couldn't believe he was not going to make it, and just wanted someone to walk out and tell me he was talking, laughing, and of course, smirking.

But that wasn't the case. After what felt like a lifetime, I entered the room, I met his grandmother, who asked a few of the players in the room to hold hands and say a prayer together. As we began to follow her lead, I became confused. "Why?" I wondered. I soon understood: it wasn't a prayer that would heal Billy in this life, but one that would take care of him in the next.

Then his parents offered me the chance to talk to him, to say good-bye. I nodded, and walked up right next to his bed. There were so many thoughts in my mind, so many questions, so many things I wanted to say—but nothing of substance came out of my mouth. He looked so peaceful, so happy. He even looked healthy. The previous morning came flooding back to me, when he was smiling, having fun, loving football, loving life. And I wiped my tears, touched his arm, smiled and said, "B.G….#29…thanks…talk to ya soon, man…love ya."

If there was anybody who hadn't realized it yet, they would find out at his funeral: Billy Gaines was a rockstar. His entire school auditorium sold out and they even had to carry the service via satellite into numerous classrooms. Strangely, it didn't feel like a funeral, it felt like a celebration. A celebration of Billy's life, Billy's impact on a small town in Maryland, Billy's ability to change many different communities, and Billy's path. It was epic.

His parents were gracious enough to offer the stage to anyone who wanted to speak. Some stories were funny, and some were sad, but all were inspiring. As I sat there with 104 other teammates and our coaching staff, I felt Billy talking to me, nudging me. "C'mon Yog, tell the story." So I waited until almost everyone had taken a turn, and then I walked what seemed like a mile toward the stage.

I had to tell the story of Billy's last day, because no one else knew it. His fans, his teammates, his family, his girlfriend and most importantly his father, who was his best friend, had to hear that Billy left this world a happy man, smiling, laughing and loving the game that brought so much joy to all of their lives.

I started slowly, but soon the story just flowed, as if Billy was right next to me. I told them how Billy was relentless in his work ethic, thrived in competitive settings, and when he was knocked down during practice, he would bounce up so fast that it looked like the grass was a springboard. And I told them that he was still rocking that old grey hoodie. Now, I'm not the most religious of people, but I do believe that when we pass away from this earth, we also return in some form. Where I always see Billy is in a game somewhere, wearing #29, and leading a team of football players whose careers on those 100 by 53 1/3 yard fields were cut short. There, B.G. is running routes, watching film, pumping his teammates up, mentoring the new members of his squad, scoring touchdowns and of course—competing. That's the only way Billy knew how to do it.

My speech wound down and I told the crowd the three sentences that have stuck with me since B.G. left us.

> *All heart and he never quit.*
> *He hated Rudy, but he loved his last day.*
> *All heart and he never quit.*

From June 18, 2003 on, every time I walk onto a football field, whether as a player at Pitt, a coach at USC, a broadcaster with Fox or ESPN, or just a fan of the game, the first thing I do is walk to the 29-yard line, put my toes on it, bend down, line up all ten fingers as if I'm catching a pass from B.G., and repeat those words.

And then I smile, a half-smile, half-smirk. Just like Billy is.

KAPPA KAPPA GAMMA

10

You guys up for a toga party? – Eric 'Otter' Stratton in "Animal House"

FINALLY, SENIOR YEAR APPROACHED, but before summer school began, I took a break for my now annual trip out west to Los Angeles and Hermosa Beach. My first year at Pitt I'd become close friends with one of the Panther tight ends, Brennan Carroll. After he graduated, he moved to L.A., where his dad, Pete Carroll, had just become head coach at the University of Southern California. He'd update me weekly on football, the beaches, the people (okay, the women...), and much more. Soon after touching down in Southern California, I'd fill up on Mexican food, jam to house music, and in general, get a taste for what life is like in Los Angeles.

During those trips I'd get to know the USC coaching staff while working their high school football camps. I would also begin to understand Pete Carroll's *Win Forever* philosophy, and embarked on what would become a lasting friendship with quarterbacks coach Steve Sarkisian. And as you might imagine, I fell for L.A. and knew I had to get back. But first, it was my senior season at Pitt.

Number one priority: find an apartment. I was on pace to graduate early and thought I might move to Australia for the spring semester. I couldn't sign a year lease with Andy and J.B., as that would leave them high and dry in the middle of the year, so I went apartment hunting in mid-July. No one could have predicted what I would stumble upon. Well, almost no one.

It was a 6-bedroom house on Atwood Street, close to campus, and the tenants needed a roommate. I met with them, even though I knew most of them already, and they checked with their parents to see if it would be okay if I moved in. After they got the green light, they left me a voicemail that I could move in immediately. Why did they have to check with their parents? Well, my soon-to-be roommates just so happened to be sisters—but not sibling sisters. No, they were sorority sisters, all five of them a part of the Kappa Kappa Gamma sisterhood, which just so happened to have the reputation as the best-looking sorority on campus.

Not only did I strike gold, as Nancy, Casey, Shonna, Lindsay and Jennifer were gorgeous, funny, and a blast to hang out with, but every single teammate lined up to help me move.

Soon our story began to sneak onto the internet. All of a sudden, college football blogs and message boards were talking about it, and we even had a segment air on Fox Sports Net that was a take-off on MTV's "Cribs." Of course, this had absolutely nothing to do with my interning at the local Fox affiliate during the year.

It was the best possible living situation I could imagine for my final months at Pitt. We had a great time living together, we laughed a lot, and, not to take anything away from my professors at Pitt, I learned plenty outside of the classroom that semester. For starters, I experienced what it was like to live with five girls, how interesting it was when I brought an "outsider" or another girl into our apartment, and how fascinating it was when I met one of their boyfriends (who rarely met with my approval) and even what it was like to say good-bye to those five awesome women. They were an important part of my Pitt family and I would do it again in a heartbeat. I can also guarantee all of my male friends would encourage it, and help me move in.

My unusual living arrangements aside, there was Pitt football to be played that year. We began the season with a win over Kent State and before I knew it, we were playing Miami at Heinz Field on Senior Night and I was running out to the 50-yard line to meet my family, give them a hug and play in my final regular season game as a Panther.

We had delivered a solid but not spectacular season as a team, although my travel roommate Larry Fitzgerald capped his year by winning every wide receiver award offered and coming so close to the Heisman Trophy that even fans outside of Pittsburgh argued that it was highway robbery.

The season ultimately had not gone as planned, as we had hopes of a BCS bowl game, but nevertheless, we would bring our best to the final test of the 2003 season—against the University of Virginia in the Continental Tire Bowl.

Heading into that last game I had never been more excited. Why? Well, I had been living and playing for the past four seasons with two clear thoughts—1) hard work always pays off, and 2) good things always happen to good people.

Maya and Ravi would say that my hard work had paid off years earlier against Bowling Green. Dad would say it was that time I called home delivering the news that I had earned a full athletic scholarship. Glenn, Woody and Vince would say that great things happened during my career as I met phenomenal friends, got out of locker 106 and lived with five sorority girls. But I disagreed. "Hard work always pays off" meant I would reach the end zone and score a Division I touchdown. "Good things always happen to good people" meant I would hand the ball to the official after making a diving catch to put six points on the board. The Cavaliers were that final opportunity and my mind was focused and at ease because, I thought, "This has to happen—I earned it."

The game got off to a fast start. But before we knew it we were deep into the fourth quarter down 23-16 with 2:28 left, and the ball on our 48-yard line. I stood on the sideline waiting to get sent into the game. "This is it," I told myself. "We'll drive down to tie the game and I'll catch the game winner!"

On first down we were sacked, fumbled the ball, and that was it.

No diving catch. No dramatic touchdown.

The feeling of our impending loss stung, but the anger that came over me was unlike anything I'd ever felt. I had to accept that I would not reach the coveted end zone in this lifetime. All I could do was watch as the clock struck :00.

After I took one last long look around Ericsson Stadium and the 51,236 fans in the stands, I let out a deep exhale and asked the football gods, "What just happened?" I entered the locker room in a daze, the loss already behind me, but I couldn't make sense of what was going on in my head. I went from lost, to angry, to emotionless, to, well… done with football.

Unlike my final game at Lackawanna Trail when we lost in the state quar-terfinals and I cried like a baby before taking off my muddy and blood-stained pads, this time I stood in front of my locker and felt nothing. My mantra, my two beliefs, my core principles had failed me—hard work *didn't* pay off and good things *didn't* happen to good people.

After I showered, tossed my helmet in my bag to take home, and said good-bye to a few teammates, I walked outside to meet my family. They were with Coach Brookhart, talking, laughing, likely saying things like "Let's stay in touch" and "Thanks for everything." It reminded me of that first day in front of Sutherland Hall—I heard nothing.

My Mom was the first one to meet me—and she instantly knew.

"I didn't score," I muttered.

"Yogi, that's true. You may not have reached the end zone during a game, but you've reached the end zone many times in the past four years."

We hugged, Coach Brookhart and I said our good-byes, and I headed for the flight back to Pennsylvania. I didn't want to talk about it, but this I knew: game over, career complete, in the blink of an eye.

My four years at Pitt seemed like four lifetimes. And when I received my degree in Communication and Rhetoric in December of 2003, I could look back on the greatest experience of my life. College football and the Pitts-burgh Panthers had given me more than just a Division I scholarship and a legitimate locker; they had given me lifelong friendships, lasting memories and another layer to the philosophical foundation already provided by my parents, my friends and the town of Dalton.

Pitt set me on a path. Where that path would lead I did not know. But I knew that by my side would be the competitive spirit and blue-collar work ethic embodied by those in the city of Pittsburgh.

I was now a proud alum, a part of the Pitt family, a graduate.

But my football career was a thing of the past. Or so I thought.

And to answer your question—no, none of the Kappa Kappa Gamma sisters and I ever dated while I lived there, honest.

LIFE ON THE WATER

11

At breakfast Anthony found a Corvette Sting Ray car kit in his breakfast cereal box and Nick found a Junior Undercover Agent code ring in his breakfast cereal box but in my breakfast cereal box all I found was breakfast cereal. I think I'll move to Australia. — Judith Viorst

DECEMBER 2003. FOOTBALL CAREER OVER. College degree attained. What the heck do I do next? After a long and intense thirty seconds of thinking, I made my decision. I took the advice of my childhood friend from Alexander and *the Terrible, Horrible, No Good, Very Bad Day*, and said, "I think I'll move to Australia."

So down under I went. I landed at Brisbane January 4, expecting to see half-dressed women jogging on bright sandy beaches, families living in grass huts, and mates surfing huge waves. No such luck, and rather perplexing. But then again, I was still at the airport. Pathetic.

Soon, though, I found my way to the Gold Coast, an hour to the south, and before long I'd made friends with a bunch of people who were also looking for somewhere to live. After ten miles of walking and searching, the eight of us found the place we would call home: 2298 Gold Coast Highway, right in the heart of Mermaid Beach. A four-bedroom, two-story house with a backyard, it was right across the street from the majestic Pacific Ocean, and not far from Surfers Paradise. Perfect.

Our new abode had only six beds. Simple math would tell you that two people were out of luck, but not for us. For starters, the two girls would be sleeping downstairs in a king-size bed together, so that left only one guy bedless. Being guys, we drew straws. And yes, I was left without a bed.

Upstairs we six guys worked it out this way: four would take the two rooms with bunk beds, and two of us took the one room in the house that had air conditioning, but just one bed. So the shortest straw had its benefits—I rotated between floor and bed, but always stayed cool.

Since we were six young strapping mates, however, there was always a chance that one of us would not sleep at our apartment due to meeting friends, locals, or even an Aussie lady. All in all, to be 22 years old and living in a coed house of eight across from the water in Australia was a pretty sweet deal. Why MTV didn't film us I have no clue.

Once I had a home, the next move was obvious—buy a surfboard. Down to the local mall I went to buy the dopest-looking 6'10" board I could find. A Jack's Surfboard, this cream-colored monster with a bamboo-like stripe down the middle was mine the minute I saw it. This baby slept in my room, got washed each night, and could probably have ordered out if she'd wanted to. I was in love.

Twenty minutes after the purchase, I was waxing it in the yard like it was a brand-new car. Twenty minutes after that I was in the ocean paddling out. Twenty minutes later I was in the ocean paddling out. Twenty minutes later I was in the ocean paddling out. Twenty minutes later....

The surfing thing looked much easier on the dvd than it was in the actual water, but I was positive I could master it. Hey, I'd been on a surfboard once before this attempt in Mermaid Beach, and I felt I was born to surf. Plus I'd watched a lot of surf videos recently: Australian pubs ran them constantly. In between downing cold VB brews, laughing with local Aussies, and attempting to chat up ridiculously good-looking surfer gals with attractive accents, I was quietly convincing myself that after a few short weeks of practice, I'd enter my first tournament. There, I would shock the surf world as I burst onto the professional tour. What could possibly go wrong?

Reality was a little different: picture some small town jock flopping in the water with a 6'10" piece of plexiglass tied to his ankle by a rope. A so-called athlete looking about as athletic as your older sister who trips while trying to walk and text at the same time. Mind you, I reference older sisters generically here; I'm not calling out any particular older sister here, Maya.

Yet my roommates also drank the Kool-Aid, and before we knew it, there were multiple boards in the house. Every morning at 4:30 (the sun comes up early over there) Nate, Justin, and I would be paddling out and getting thrashed. Three or four hours later, we'd be starving, and we'd break for a breakfast burrito. At 10:00, back in the water. And by noon, home for a few PB&J's and a nap. By 3:00 in the afternoon we were throwing the football around, and later, Nate and I hit the water again to watch the sun set right in front of us. (Justin refused to surf after 6:00 p.m. because, as he so elegantly stated, "Sharks have to eat too.") Then we'd sit around, relax, and tell stories before hitting the local spots on a search for our future wives, who would obviously give us surfing lessons.

After a few weeks of partying and surfing, I was missing something—and naturally, I thought it was ball. Football had been such a major part of my life for so long that it was hard to break away. I had time on my hands, no visible income, and didn't really know what to do with myself. So I returned to the gridiron with the Gold Coast Stingrays, one of a growing number of teams Down Under that play American football.

The Stingrays were mostly locals from 18 to 45 years old, and mostly out of shape, but their love for the game of football was unmatched. They would watch NFL games at 3:00 a.m., prepare for their ESPN fantasy draft as if they were each Todd McShay, and talk more ball than I would ever want to. And that's saying something.

We practiced a few nights a week and held inter-squad scrimmages. It was a blast, not only because they were great blokes, but also because I felt like a Heisman Trophy winner as I ran routes against 35-year-old cornerbacks.

But the football career in Australia didn't bring the satisfaction I'd felt playing Division I ball at Pitt. I knew I needed something more. So I hit the road.

This time I wasn't alone. I had met "the one." Stunningly beautiful, she told me she was Hawaiian. Blond and blue-eyed, well tanned, great smile—I hadn't been to Hawaii since I was 10 years old, but I could just picture her laying out on Waikiki Beach.

Our ten-day trek began in Melbourne, where we watched the Australian Open. Roger Federer was playing in the quarterfinals, and after his win, he tossed his wristband into the stands—directly into my hands. This had to mean good luck or something. We then took a trip along the Great Ocean Road, stopping in villages and farms. Adelaide was our final stop, and from its name to its culture, I fell in love instantly.

But sadly, the girl I had so easily fallen for a week-and-a-half earlier turned out not to be "the one." It seems that, although she was born in Hawaii, she was raised in Ohio. Big difference. Unless I heard her wrong the first time. Ohioan, Hawaiian—who can be sure?

In any case, on to Sydney. From there, Jerome, another Mermaid Beach roommate, and I flew into the heart of the outback, to what is known as Australia's Red Centre. The central Australian desert has been home to the continent's Aborigines for around 50,000 years; Alice Springs, the main city of about 25,000 people, has a thriving indigenous art community, and a fairly busy tourist trade. But the surrounding landscape is also extremely dry, insanely hot and full of nothing but sand and a big rock, known as Ayers Rock.

So that's where we went. In Alice Springs, Jerome and I rented a white two-door Honda Civic and began the drive to Ayres Rock, or, as the locals call it, Uluru. For five hours we drove along the desert road, through a landscape that was both desolate and magnificent; with each mile we told ourselves our burdens were lifting, our spirits soaring, but mostly we were trying to find a good song on the radio to fill in the silences. You can only talk so much.

Then, after rounding the final bend, we witnessed what has to be one of the most astonishing sights on earth. Uluru. Just as *Lonely Planet* had stated, the colors of this gigantic rock transformed with each passing minute, from red to orange to purple. It was captivating, mesmerizing.

Before we got to the campground, we pulled over and I jumped in the Civic's trunk because Jerome and I were too broke to afford two entry tickets. Once we arrived at the base of Uluru, we agreed that we would not climb it out of respect for the locals, who consider it a sacred site.

That pledge lasted about a minute. We had not flown 1500 miles and driven six hours in the hot desert just to look at a big rock. We were definitely climbing this bad boy.

Up we went. First, we climbed with the rest of the tourists up a steep incline alongside a chain that stretched for 200 meters. At the top of the chain, Jerome and I shot glances at each other and took off like 10-year olds, never looking back. We jumped up and down craters, we leapt over streams, we ducked under boulders—and we separated, climbing solo, each looking for the route that would take us to the top fastest.

On one side of us was the bright orange setting sun, and on the other, the cool blue of the rising moon. With every step, Uluru would reveal a new hue—I felt somehow that this huge desert was wrapping me in its arms, making me feel I belonged here.

Finally, at the peak of Uluru, sunset and moonrise met. Jerome and I stared transfixed, as the sun and moon came closer to each other, briefly nodding, seemingly only yards from each other, then passed like two old friends. It was if the cosmos took a little pause, a tiny breath, and then moved on.

It was a powerful moment for both of us—we felt so insignificant in the face of it, like two tiny grains of sand in this desert that stretched on forever. But we recovered rapidly, and decided to reclaim our place in the universe. We snapped some pictures, then shot video of each of us there at the top of the world, delivering ultra-serious and meaningful monologues on the sun, the moon, the earth, and us. Of course we got totally mocked by Nate, Justin, and the other guys back at the house—for basically being so dramatic out there in the midst of that amazing natural beauty, and filming it. We probably also weren't helped much by my small-town Pennsylvania accent and Jerome's thick Bostonian twang. "Aces, baby, all aces." He actually said that.

Then we began the trek—or shall I say, the slide—back, as we cruised down Uluru on our backsides. On the way, we kept seeing this one particular set of high beams moving throughout the park. Oops—visitors were not allowed to sleep near Uluru, and Jerome and I had overstayed our welcome. Someone was looking for us.

To former jocks, though, this was a competition: our goal was to stay in the park for the night, but to avoid authority at all costs. We hurried to the parking lot, making our plans along the way.

We hightailed out of there in our white getaway Civic. Around the park we sped, hiding in corners with our headlights off, parking behind bushes, and basically being Jack Bauer before Kiefer Sutherland knew who Jack Bauer was. It was a brilliant plan until we got tired. Finding a secluded spot, we parked the car for the night, calculating that we needed to sleep for only two hours, as the sun would be rising at 5:00 a.m., and we wanted to witness Uluru and all its colors at dawn.

At 4:30 a.m. I awoke to a flashlight in my face.

Busted.

It was the park ranger and he was not too happy with us. Thankfully, my communication and rhetoric degree from Pitt helped out, and he let us go after a stern talking-to. Crisis averted. We returned to the Gold Coast without an Aussie arrest record, thankfully.

After Uluru, I headed to Tasmania to visit my relatives.

Uncle Myles and his wife and children live on the island in a tiny town of approximately twenty families. He is a former Navy officer who lived underwater for many years on a submarine, so it's no surprise he's kind of cerebral. When he opens up, though, he's very easy to like.

Tazzie, as it's called, was fascinating for its unique culture and setting, so isolated from the rest of the world. Its people are old-fashioned, family-oriented, and will often keep the same house for generations. For such a small state, Tasmania has a vast and spectacular landscape that made me feel like I was Frodo Boggins in *The Lord of the Rings*.

Each morning I would go for a run through fields of bulls, horses, and other animals. One particular morning, though, something came over me as I ran. In an instant, my wind was taken from me. I gasped for air, as the oxygen was sucked from my lungs. Panic turned to euphoria, oddly, my lungs suddenly opened up, and my legs became light as feathers. I didn't know what was wrong with me, but I put it out of my mind and cruised back to Myles' house and got ready for our day trip to Hobart.

After walking around the city for a few hours, I decided to call home on a pay phone across from the capitol building. Before I even heard the dial tone, I knew something had happened. Mom answered on the first ring. She was brief.

"Baba passed away earlier today."

Not being one to wear emotions on my sleeve, I told my Aunt Annette the news, and we went about the rest of our day in Hobart. When we arrived back at their home, Myles asked me to go outside. I met him in the backyard, and gazed over lush green fields that seemed endless. Myles made idle chit-chat for a while, then handed me an axe and asked me to split some logs for firewood. Half-heartedly I took it and began hacking away.

With each swing I became angrier. Angry with Myles for asking me to split wood after I just found out my grandmother had died. Angry with myself for not being in the States for the service. Angry with God for taking my mom's mentor away. Just angry.

After about 45 minutes of furious log splitting and talking to myself, I stopped. Out of breath, I put my foot up on a stack of wood and gazed out over the rolling hills of Tasmania. And I started to laugh.

Myles, an emotional tactician if there ever was one, knew that the simple task of log splitting would allow me to blow off some steam and think about my grandmother, regardless of how irritated I was initially. Well done, Myles. I felt a lot better. And I'm sure the extra firewood helped him out, too.

When I returned to Mermaid Beach, my camera was full, but my bank account was empty. And so my successful career at the local mall as an internet kiosk employee began, along with a rice and water diet. Actually, it was more like a cleanse. Four weeks later, I was a master at creating new Hotmail and Yahoo e-mail accounts for older European and Asian tourists and about fifteen pounds lighter.

But still, I was missing something.

So I went surfing. Alone. No Nate, no Justin, no Jerome. Just me and my board. And that particular morning in the water, something came over me more powerful than a six-foot wave. For two hours I sat on my board watching the sunrise, seagulls, and surfers. That was when I figured it out.

Life.

That morning I figured out life.

As the sun rose slowly out of the Pacific, I realized that life is simple. As simple as a sunrise and a sunset, a smile and a handshake, a hug and a kiss, a log and an axe. We humans make it complex. We take simple issues and turn them into huge ordeals. We get frustrated when we don't make a catch or score a touchdown. We think that our world is going to end when we lose a job, girlfriend, or family member. In reality, when things happen, both good and bad, that's life. And life is full of choices. We choose to be happy. We choose to be angry. We choose to be positive or negative. That morning, on my cream-colored Jack's Surfboard with the bamboo-like stripe down the middle, life became simple. What scientists, mystics, mathematicians, theoretical physicists, and yes, yogis, have been trying to figure out for centuries, I got in mere seconds.

When you surf, a lot of thoughts run through your mind. That morning, after I split the atom of life, I began to think about my old girl, my family, and, of course, Baba. She used to ask, "How's your girlfriend?" My response, from the time I was 4 years old, had been the same: "Which one?" A funny joke that we had both enjoyed for eighteen years now brought a smile the size of Uluru to my face. Don't get the wrong idea: Baba wasn't trying to tell me that it was okay to have ten girlfriends. Rather, she was telling me to surround myself with love.

After graduating college, I once had asked her for girl advice. In her soft yet distinct Polish accent, she had said that if the girl was playing games with me to forget her, but if I loved her with all my heart and soul, I should go get her and never look back. She then had grasped my hands and looked me in the eyes. "Yogi, pain will heal. If you do not love, then life is not worth living.... Life is nothing without love."

At the time, her advice didn't really register, but in the water on that memorable morning, the words "Life is nothing without love" knocked me over with the power of a great white.

I couldn't get off the beach fast enough. I jogged back to the house, board under my arm, and did the one thing I felt I should do.

Write.

Run-on sentences, incomplete thoughts, passionate paragraphs, journal entries, and stories flowed from my fingers. Creativity was my new drug. I cannot say if any of my writing was any good, but at least it was therapeutic. And I needed that.

Through my writing, I finally began to recognize that I was more than a helmet and shoulder pads. I was more than the punk high school freshman who'd flipped out on his senior captain. I was more than the college freshman who'd talked his way onto the travel squad. Football was not who I was—football was what I did. Who I was—a work in progress, I guess. But this I knew: deep inside me beat the heart of the competitor who'd grown up on the Dalton Courts with a thirst for adventure, and a need to do everything better than it had ever been done before.

IS THAT PIG KOSHER?

12

SO I WENT WITH MY NEW PASSION. Getting in the water. Surfing hits you physically, mentally and spiritually, and I was lucky enough to be someplace where I could do it all the time. So I spent my days popping up on my board for the mythical pro tour—true, I started out pretty bad, but I was getting better day by day, in preparation for a surfing junket Nate and I had planned for Bali, Indonesia.

Sometimes, just for an extra challenge, we'd hit the waves during a tropical storm, just to see if we could handle it. Our last day in Australia, there I was at dusk, alone in the water, with Jerome watching from shore. The previous day's storm had produced the best waves I'd seen in Australia, so I paddled out, and somehow caught a 10' wave that was, no lie, the biggest I had ever witnessed—and I managed to ride it to the sand. Totally jacked, I jumped back in the water. As soon as the next decent-sized wave came, I charged. Before I knew what was happening, my board slipped out from under me and smashed me right between the eyes. I went underwater for a second, but quickly climbed up my leash to rest on my board. That's when I noticed a little blood, so I headed back in. Somehow I made it to shore and staggered up to Jerome, who took one look at my cut and said, "Duuude, that's wicked deep. I think I can see your brains."

The lifeguard had no gauze, and really no emergency care supplies of any kind. The only thing he had was a good quote, "Mate, that's quite deep," which I already knew. Thanks. So we headed off for the nearest medical facility a few miles away. By the time we got there, I was looking even more roughed up, and the admitting nurse was really sympathetic. "Oh, dear," she said, "You've really gone and done it, haven't you? Too bad our good surgeon just left for the day. But don't you worry, we'll find someone to fix you up as good as new."

Seven messy stitches later, I was on my way. They gave me ointment to cover the wound, told me to be extra-careful touching my face, and were very clear that under no circumstances should I go in the water until two weeks had passed and the stitches were removed by a qualified physician. Otherwise I would be left with a massive scar.

I made it for two days. Day one Nate and I flew to Bali, and day two I watched him surf. That night we found some old shears somewhere, sterilized them with rubbing alcohol and matches, and then anesthetized me with a couple of Bintangs. Dr. Nate performed the surgery, the stitches were gone, and I was back in the water.

We were spending our first four nights in an awesome resort right near where the nightclub bombing had taken place some eighteen months before. Rates were rock-bottom, the local markets were struggling, and the economy was sluggish at best. Everything was dirt cheap in this third world country, but even so, we were short of cash, so we moved into a local hostel and snuck back into our former hotel every morning for their free breakfast. And truthfully, we also popped in there for the staff, who were quite attractive.

It was the total beach life. We'd surf all day and half the night, and Nate would go spearfishing and cook our dinner over an open fire. Three hours of sleep and we'd be back at it the next day.

The best break in Bali was at an island just offshore, so one day we took a boat out there to stay for a few days. We stayed in beach huts, hit the water every chance we had, and explored the tiny island in our off time. One afternoon I took a jog and ended up in a little shop filled with figurines.

"What are these?" I asked.

"Yogis," came the reply.

I chose one and showed it to him. "This is a yogi? Yogi—that's my name."

The shopkeeper looked at me like I was crazy. After seeing my passport, though, he nodded, smiled, and said softly, "Yogi, we've been waiting for you."

He then picked up each yogi in the shop and told me its story—and by the end, I understood that Yogi meant a man of sound mind, body and soul. Pretty cool.

For a month Nate and I surfed, read, and hung with the locals, who were amazing. Standing no taller than maybe 4' 8", and model skinny, they radiated happiness, and it was rubbing off on me. The peaceful Balinese culture brought out my more meditative, contented side, but I also knew that I needed one more trip before returning to Pennsylvania. The islands of Fiji fit the bill.

This time I'd be going solo. Nate would remain in Australia for another month, while I flew to Fiji. And that first night in Nadi, where the airport is, suggested an adventure of a really different kind. I landed with $40 to my name, and one goal: to surf at Sigatoka. Huge Fijian men twice my size stared me down as I walked through total darkness trying to find the local hostel. In Bali, of course, I'd been a giant. Here, I was tiny. It was a little bit unnerving, actually. I finally made it to the hostel, plunked down $2 for a dorm bed, and discovered the place was virtually empty. It was also pitch-black—they turned off the electricity at ten o'clock. I spooned my board all night long. Not saying I was scared—I was just cautious.

First thing the next morning I hitched a ride south; I was headed for Sigatoka's famous beach break near Club Mesa. My ride dropped me off and I explored for a while, eventually finding a hostel, but after careful consideration of my finances (or lack thereof), I decided to wait for a while. That's when a large Fijian approached me.

"Bula vinaka," he said.

"Bula vinaka," I replied. It's a friendly greeting. So far, so good.

"You look for surfing?"

"Yes," I admitted.

"My sons will take you. Come stay with us."

Taken aback, I gave a quiet but grateful "No thanks" and continued on my way. Not that I was intimidated or anything, but this guy was as big as an NFL linebacker.

Minutes later, as I was wandering through Sigatoka carefully planning the next few hours of my life (in other words, wondering what the heck to do…), the same guy suddenly materialized right next to me. "Sir, are you sure? My sons can take you surfing. Come to my home."

I took a minute to ponder this, then I decided to take Tom Cruise's advice in *Risky Business*: "Sometimes you've just got to say 'What the f***.'" So I hopped in the back of his mini dump truck, along with my board, and gazed at the lush vegetation as we sped along. I relaxed, took a few deep breaths of that soft fragrant air, and let my mind ease. Life was again good.

For a few minutes, that is, life was good. Then the truck suddenly lurched off-road into the jungle, and civilization simply vanished. I could see nothing—just the rutted road we bounced over. I figured this was the end of Yogi: they'd never find my body, because the bones would have been picked clean by ravenous jungle animals. Bats and bugs would finish the job. Hey, if you're gonna die in an exotic location, at least make it memorable.

After a couple of miles of kidney-punishing bumps, we came to an abrupt halt. The jungle just opened up, and a perfect little village was laid out in front of me as if it had been painted there. I hopped out of the back and saw that every eye was on me. Tata, my kidnaper-slash-host, smiled broadly and welcomed me to his village. Next he proudly introduced the Vanai-Siliwais family of eight: Nasoni and Esave were his boys; Sula, Akenetea, and Makirina were his daughters. Tata's wife Nana and grandmother Tai Yalewa stood behind them.

As they dressed me in a sarong (there are no pictures of this, so visualize if you must) and walked me to the town dining hall, I realized I was in for some sort of party.

Apparently Mother's Day is an international holiday—because that's what they were gathering to celebrate. They had no tables and no chairs, but three colorful table runners lined the floor, with food arranged in the center. Families sat alongside it, and ate yams, baked bananas, and fruit. My memory is a little fuzzy on the details, perhaps because of the kava that was being passed around.

Kava was a new experience, and the locals enjoyed my first sip. As I held the bowl, thirty sets of eyes were glued to my every move. I analyzed the grey liquid, wondering if it was dirty tap water, Fijian tea, or some drug that would eventually leave me naked on the roadside without my $40, which was now $38.

But c'mon, what choice did I really have?

So down the hatch it went. I tried to be cool, to play it off, but my look of surprise gave me away. This stuff was strong—and the psychoactive effects were quite pleasant, and immediate. The locals totally cracked up.

My second day in the village, Nasovi took me to Suva, the capitol and largest city. The bus ride was long and loud, filled with people and poultry—everyone was pretty rowdy as they set out for a day's business, and they had to holler to be heard over the constant squawking of the chickens headed for market. After our ears stopped ringing, we walked around town for a while and then sat down to talk at an old park bench overlooking the ocean. We shared a loaf of French bread as Nasovi told me about the government and the coup that had occurred a few years earlier. Soldiers with machine guns had roamed the streets, and I could tell he feared for those he loved, and that he wanted to help his people. He stared into the ocean and slowly revealed his dreams for peace and health for his family. His mother and sister had recently fallen sick and couldn't afford a doctor, but Nasovi trusted that love and God would heal them both. He knew, though, that he had a deep responsibility to all of them and by extension, society. The Vanai-Siliwais epitomized the concept of family—and Tata proved that, as I found out later that he had worked Nasovi's shift that night so that I'd have a guide in Suva.

On the bus ride back, the world seemed quieter. The locals were chatting back and forth idly, and even the few surviving chickens had stopped their squawking. It was as if the life around me had found its balance between mind, body, and soul, and I was living in a state of "divine nonchalance."

When we got back, Nana and her youngest daughter were really very sick—it seemed like some kind of flu, maybe, but I was worried, and gave them my aspirin to bring down their fevers. It bothered me that I couldn't do more—they'd been so generous to me.

Pretty soon, though, I was in one of the other rooms, laughing with Esave, his cousin Kitone, and their two friends, Asaeli and Tubili. The boys had a ritual of giving each other American nicknames such as "Cartoon Boy" or "William," so they quickly dubbed me "Big Boss Man." Kitone and I turned this into a skit: he'd flex his muscles and say, "You Big Boss Man," and I would flex back, responding, "You Small Boss Man." Ah, it was great to be 8 years old again.

The whole evening they kept begging me, "Tell a story." They were on the edges of their seats in anticipation—and the guy who had stories from

Dalton to Pitt to Australia just blanked. Eventually I came up with something lame about New York City, and some adventure/mishap there, and they watched me intently while hanging on every word. The night ended with Esave and me singing our respective national anthems. He nailed it, while I had a little trouble with the high notes. And as he sang to us, his voice bursting with pride for his people, I teared up a little. We didn't even realize that their grandmother was standing just outside the cinderblock room the whole time. After Esave's song, she called me into the main room. There she presented me with a gift, a small painting she'd made. When I asked if there was a spiritual meaning to it, she smiled and said no, but I disagreed. For her and her family of eight, giving was spiritual, and they thought first about the happiness of their guest before they considered their own. That night, a bond was created between a family and a foreigner—and I knew that bond would stick with us.

For the next few days I hung out with every villager I could find, asking questions and listening to their stories. No surprise, but the children affected me the most. During the day, they would teach me how to climb coconut trees and use a machete in the jungle. At night, I would teach them English nouns, vowels, and sentence structure before finishing with a story from the U.S.

On my final morning I awoke to the horrible cacophony of roosters crowing. Don't the hens get sick of this day after day? Trust me, no matter how much serenity one feels, roosters will always be loud and annoying.

I immediately noticed the pace outside was different—the village was up to something. Tata was digging a hole and Nasovi and Esave were piling up kindling, wood, and rocks. When I asked Sula what was going on, she told me that the village was having a ceremonial meal in my honor. Embarrassed, I went outside to help with the preparations.

Once the hole was dug and the kindling lit, the boys and I laid large, circular rocks upon a fire pit to act as hot coals. Then Esave picked up a heavy three-foot log and climbed over a small fence into a pigpen. When Tata pointed at one of the pigs, Esave started taking batting practice at its head. The smack of log hitting cranium was both hollow and piercing, and I was shocked and even a little sick. Well, a lot sick—I was raised a vegetarian, had experimented with chicken wings in high school and chicken-and-rice bowls in college, and had my first experience eating fish with Nate in Bali. But this was different.

Once the poor little fellow was unconscious, or at least severely concussed, Esave dragged it to the fire pit, where his or her legs were tied together. Then the boys took turns sawing at its throat and burning the hair from its pink body. That pig was the toughest animal I'd ever seen: it simply refused to die. While it oinked and squealed, I had to walk away for fear of vomiting on the animal being murdered in my honor.

When it was time to eat, villagers kept bringing in food at different times. I felt uncomfortable as those who prepared the food didn't even get to enjoy it. Did I eat the pig? No. I just couldn't do it. It was presented beautifully, wrapped up in a pretty green leaf, but every time I looked at it, I saw the image of Esave doing his best Aaron Boone 2003 World Series impersonation, and that hollow sound rang in my ears.

After the meal, it was time to say so-long and thank you. Sad, yes, but the goodbye hugs and kisses were full of joy. This Fijian village had turned my life upside down. The Vanai-Siliwai family had taken me in, a tourist with a surfboard, and put a roof over my head and too much food in my belly. Their happiness, laughter, and love for one another were contagious. Negative thoughts had no place in this village, and Tata, who worked from 7:00 p.m. to 7:00 a.m., or Nasovi, who worked from 6:00 a.m. to 6:00 p.m, never complained. When they came home each day, their beautiful smiles stretched from ear to ear as they greeted their loved ones.

Those six months in the South Pacific changed my life forever. On the flight to Los Angeles, I reviewed and relived my trip as I jotted thoughts in my journal, but I also found myself looking ahead—perhaps to some terrific job, to future travels, but mostly, to all the gifts life would offer, as something good was surely just about to happen.

As my plane touched down for my West Coast stopover, I put away my pen and began to focus on my next move. At that moment, the woman who had sat next to me the entire flight spoke for the first time.

"Maybe you should write a book," she said.

Maybe I already am, I thought, but first I should thank Alexander (and his terrible, horrible, no good, very bad day).

STYLE, VISION, THEME

13

Now life is a gamble… and that's the fun part. – *Coach Pete Carroll*

I WAS HUNGRY FOR SOME WEST COAST CULTURE at this point, so I'd planned a quick stop in L.A. before getting back to Pennsylvania. Brennan picked me up at the airport and we headed south to Hermosa Pier, where he grilled me about what had transpired Down Under. "Details, bro… details," he said. I left out the part about the enormous Fijians, but was fairly honest about life on the Gold Coast and all it offered. Then I had dinner with his dad, Pete Carroll, in a beachside hangout, just to catch up, and to talk a little ball. Pretty much the best possible reintroduction to life in the States.

Plus I needed a couple of days to clean up—I'd been a beach bum for six months, and it showed. Once I was fairly presentable, I flew back to Dalton, just to see if I had changed as much as I thought I had.

Instead I transformed into that post-college guy who lives at home, goes out with his boys to reminisce, and plays hoops on Wednesday nights with the 40-year-old hometown guys. After four weeks of that, I went stir crazy and hopped into a car with Vince and drove cross-country—and back again. We tried to convince Glenn and Woody to join us, but Glenn was starting his fifth year of what would be a five-and-a-half year undergrad experience, and Woody was starting law school in New York City. So from Dalton to Savannah and New Orleans to L.A., Vince and I rocked out to Aerosmith, George Strait, and my crush at the time—Jessica Simpson. Then it was Utah to North Dakota, back through Colorado, and over to Niagara Falls before returning to Dalton on July 3rd, 2004—all with two surfboards strapped to the roof of Vince's magenta Mazda 626. We hit twenty-seven states in twenty-six days, slept in Vince's ride, and bickered over who'd drive and who'd make the PB & J's on rice cakes. An epic trip, and worth every penny, even though we never got our boards in the water.

By now I was really broke. I'd interned at Fox Sports Net Pittsburgh during college, and I still had a few connections. So I packed up my Toyota Tercel and headed to Pittsburgh, where I signed on with both Fox and the Pitt Panthers radio network as a sideline reporter, radio host, and studio analyst. If you had asked me, I'd have said I had the best job in the world—talking sports, going to games, and getting paid for it. I was no Milton Waddams in *Office Space*, spending fifteen hours a day in a cubicle typing up TPS reports and protecting my red stapler. No, I was on the air—and talking about football. Sure, I wouldn't be making much money, but I didn't need to, since I was sleeping on my college roommate J.B. Gibboney's couch and eating like a bird.

Before my first season as a real live broadcaster, I went to New York City to meet one of Coach Carroll's best friends, Pat Kirwan, who worked for the NFL Network. We were just getting out of a cab on the corner of Park Avenue and East 41st St. when he asked me what my on-air style was going to be. With so much college ball in my recent past, I had the answer: "I'm going to be like Kirk Herbstreit, you know, give a former player's perspective."

Pat, one of the nicest but most brutally honest people I've ever met, all but laughed in my face. Then he patiently explained, "Yogi, before you get on air, you need to have a style, a vision, and theme. Know who you are as a person and what you want to represent on air. If not, you'll get eaten alive when Pitt loses and you will never gain your peers' respect." Frankly, at the time I didn't really get it. But I thought I'd give it a try.

Over the next thirty days, I began to search for my style, vision, and theme. First I had to figure out what they actually were, and then I'd get to work finding them. Style? That one was easy—it's the personal qualities you bring to whatever you do. Vision is again fairly simple—it's the goal, it's what you are setting out to do. And theme, well, that's the way you live your life, day to day—your belief system. Definitions, check. As to how they all applied to me personally, that was the tough part.

So I sat in my dad's home office in front of his computer and wrote. And wrote and wrote. Run-on sentences, bullet points, whole paragraphs, it didn't matter. And like when I came off the beach in Australia after a surf, I thought I'd nailed it. So I sent a 28-page attachment off to Pat via e-mail. His response was simple: "Good start; now cut it down to one sentence." Back to the Dell I went, and hit delete. Again and again. Finally I was left with just the essentials. It was lean, it was tight, it was the start of answering some really tough questions about myself.

By the time the season began, I had some sense of the type of reporter I wanted to be and the style in which I would analyze the game. I'd bring energy and focus to the task, I'd challenge conventional wisdom, and I'd bring everything I'd ever experienced as a player to my new role as an analyst. And I'd separate fact from opinion. The first few games were easy, because Pitt won, and my post-game questions revolved around their stellar defense and the star quarterback, Tyler Palko, one of my closest friends. In the fifth game of the season, though, Pitt was beaten by lowly Connecticut, and my style was tested.

Head Coach Walt Harris was taking heavy criticism for the loss, but just because I was his friend and former player, I couldn't be a homer. I had to ask the hard questions, no matter the consequences. And during his press conference that following Monday, I did just that.

Pitt's third down success rate had been poor in that game compared to the previous three games, and I had noticed a change in personnel. So I asked him about it: "Coach, in the first three games your third-down success rate was over 50% and you were typically in three wide sets. This past game your third-down percentage was well below average and you were in base personal most of the time. Why the change?"

Coach Harris was noticeably aggravated with me as he formulated his answer—and as the new guy in the room, I felt like the heat had just been cranked up. When I walked out of the press conference, Rob King, one of my first mentors in the media, pulled me aside and said, "Good question, man. Way to stick with the facts."

It was a proud moment for me: I had stood by the style I had developed over the summer—I would be the young, energetic analyst who asked questions based on what actually happened in the game, not what I would have done if I were the head coach. I knew that Coach Harris might be upset with me, but I had a job to do. Fact, not fantasy—that's what being a college football analyst is. At least to me. And for the record, Coach Harris later praised my research, and we continued a friendship that remains extremely strong today.

From that day on, I believed I could be successful in any profession if I remained true to my style. I also saw that having a backbone is not just helpful, but absolutely necessary for success in the media.

That football season, Rob and I teamed up to deliver a successful call-in show. By the time hoops began in winter, Fox Sports brought me in studio as a football and basketball analyst, and then gave me the chance of a lifetime: hosting my own post-game basketball call-in show. During those few months of the season, our show went from a listenership of about ten (and I knew them all personally) to thousands. Together we'd all talk sports at a rapid clip, and of course, argue. The most hilarious thing was having my opinions challenged live, by a mix of armchair quarterbacks, special guests, friends, and even family. Sometimes I won, sometimes I lost, but I was always smiling. Who could ask for a better gig?

One day near the end of basketball season, as I was sitting in my makeshift office, I got a phone call. My gut told me who it was, even though I didn't recognize the number. To voicemail it went, and the message was simple.

"Hey, man, it's M.J. I know you have a lot going on but we might have an opening out here if you're interested. Give me a shout back when you get a sec." M.J. was Mark Jackson, a great friend of mine, who worked at the University of Southern California with Coach Carroll.

I loved my work in the media and knew I'd gotten my dream job, but when that call came in from California, I could almost taste the salt water. If you've ever surfed, you know how addictive it is, that euphoria that takes hold of you at sunrise as you sprint into the ocean with a board under your arm, and that rush of standing on a board enveloped by the hollow sound of the green room. All the way from Pittsburgh I could feel the strong pull of the ocean, and I longed for that peace and spiritual connection that the art of surfing provides.

So I called M.J. back.

He explained the scenario and the offer. I didn't let on, but he could have told me that I would be lining the practice field, and I would have considered it—the ocean meant that much to me.

Later that same evening, I was walking into the Omni Hotel to meet my friend Bo Garrett, when my cell phone rang again. Another number I didn't recognize, but I answered it this time.

"Hey, Yog. It's Pete. How are you, man?"

"Coach, what's going on?"

"So are you coming to work for us or what? Let's go, man, you need to get out to L.A. and get back in the water."

The man knew just what to say to me. *Play it cool, Yog, play it cool.* "Mmm... yeah, Coach, I spoke with Mark earlier and would love to discuss it further with you."

"Okay, call me tomorrow, but not too early. I'm sleeping in."

"Okay, talk to you later."

Perfect timing, these phone calls. If I could pick anyone to bounce this thing off of, it'd be Bo. He worked at ESPN and had a solid business head on his shoulders. For two hours, we talked about the pros of going to Los Angeles and the cons of leaving the local media industry, where I was having success in a top twenty-five market at the ripe old age of 23. After a few beers and one too many handfuls of salty cashews, it all seemed clear. A job in the media wasn't going away, but the opportunity at USC wouldn't last forever. And I remembered the career advice Coach Carroll had offered me when I'd met him for dinner nine months ago back in Hermosa Beach. "Well, Yogi, now life is a gamble...and that's the fun part."

So I made my decision: L.A., not PA., at least for the time being. My goal was to fill up my brain as much as possible, earn a master's degree from USC's Annenberg School of Communication, and return to the media a few years later with much more to offer. Call me competitive, but I wanted to have the sharpest skills of any sports analyst around.

So west I went. A flight to Los Angeles, no matter the departure point, is a one-of-a-kind experience. Every conceivable type of person is on that plane, and they all seem to have a special light in their eyes, as if they're traveling into the future or something. It's exhilarating. But as I landed in Los Angeles, something else came over me, a feeling I'd never really felt before.

Excitement and eagerness, of course, but also a sense of being home. Weird. I had never lived in L.A. before, but my gut instinct told me this was where I'd find some missing piece of myself. Sure, the Pacific Ocean was beckoning to me, wave after wave, but it was far more than that. L.A. is full of dreamers, full of people who have moved out west from Iowa, or Vermont, or Pennsylvania, because L.A. stimulates their creativity and ignites their ambition, allowing them to flourish and expand like no other place on earth. And now, for the first time, as I walked off the plane at LAX, I too was living in the land of dreamers.

Minutes later, I looked back into the terminal at the sign that said "I Love L.A." Then I took a deep breath of the salty air, looked up at the palm trees swaying in the ocean breeze, and felt that something was very right.

PART II
...to LA

HOLLYWOOD

14

BRENNAN MET ME CURBSIDE, all dark shades and hip-hop.
"Glad you finally figured it out."

Typical Brennan. He made short work of the chaotic LAX traffic and within minutes we were beachside in Hermosa. Home sweet home, at least for the time being.

Now Brennan, or B.C., is my closest friend other than the three boys from Dalton, a guy who can make you laugh even when you don't think you have it in you. He's loyal to a fault—a quality you appreciate when you're one of his friends, and a quality you regret if you cross one of those friends. He also has a need to make occasions memorable—again, a quality that usually is awesome, but sometimes, not so much. And at this moment, he wanted to make sure that my introduction to life in Los Angeles was one that I would not soon forget.

B.C.'s roommate Jaycon, another friend from Pitt, was a nightclub manager who had the hook-up everywhere we went. So night one, they took me out clubbing in Hollywood, and we ended up at one of the town's hottest spots. The doorman recognized Jaycon immediately, brought us to the front of the line, and told us that we were in—but that there was some kind of special private VIP party going on as well. He gave us no details, though, so I was thinking, hmmm, movie celebrities, industry movers and shakers, not so bad for being one day out of PA.

We got inside and that's when I began to rethink. First, I noticed a couple of women making out with each other. And then another couple of women. Also, there seemed to be some sort of holiday theme going on. What on earth was happening here?

After closer inspection, we discovered that the VIP's were a group of individuals who make their living taking off their clothes on camera. Or to put it more bluntly, we'd stumbled into a Christmas party for porn stars, in the middle of February. Surreal. No way was I getting anywhere near Santa, but Mrs. Claus and the female elves were kinda cute.

Meanwhile, we mixed and mingled with the rest of the crowd, who seemed pretty uninterested in what was going on across the room. The evening was full of celebratory cheers, laughs, and "Hi, I'm new here" introductions. Of course, like any newbie from the East Coast, I fell in love with the first girl I laid eyes on. As we spent the night dancing, laughing, and watching the world of Hollywood XXX entertainment unfold before our eyes, my smooth moves were working on her like magic.

The next day I went to the local bar where she worked. Confident as *Entourage's* Vinnie Chase at Teddy's, I walked up to her and tapped her on the shoulder. She turned, looked at me as if I were some yahoo from, I dunno, the backwoods of Pennsylvania, and said, "Um…who are you?" And that's when I shrank from 5'11' to 2'11". I've told myself countless times that she didn't recognize me because I was wearing my contacts instead of the glasses I wore to the club, and thus, looked even cooler than the night before.

So I went from PA to L.A. in less than six hours, my welcoming party was crashed by the porn industry and their holiday bash, I fell in love with a beautiful blond only to be crushed by her the following day, and I drank more Grand Marnier than I thought humanly possible.

But I was in L.A. The weekend ended, and my first day on the job approached. I woke up extra early, took a warm shower, pounded a few Gatorades (like you've never done that), and threw on my slacks and button-down.

M.J. met me at the office and gave me the rundown.

Well, after he made me tell him about my weekend.

NINETEEN SECONDS

15

19 seconds will never define you. – *Coach Pete Carroll*

I STOOD ON THE SC INTERLOCK in the lobby of Heritage Hall, on that massive cardinal carpet with the gold letters, and took it all in. Heisman Trophies, National Championship crystal balls, retired jerseys and more surrounded me, and I felt a surge of adrenaline that took me back five years to the steps of Sutherland Hall in Pittsburgh. I was about to begin a new journey, and this one would be at one of the most historic institutions in the world—as part of a program that had changed the college football landscape like no other in recent history. Needless to say, I was jacked.

Slacks pressed, shirt tucked in, notepad under my arm, and pen in pocket I arrived in M.J.'s office ready to learn player personnel, recruiting and, I hoped, the secret to USC's success. We talked for a few hours before he took me around to meet the rest of the staff—who instantly demanded I untuck my shirt and lose the slacks for shorts, or at least jeans. I got that the rhythm here would be a bit different, and I soon found it: wake up early, carpool with B.C., read the *LA Times*, arrive at the office, learn as much from M.J. as possible, and race to the beach for a sunset surf. And that rhythm would last all of two weeks.

I was in the copy room one morning when Coach Carroll called out, "Yogi, come on into my office."

As we walked down the hall, he said, "I know you said you didn't want to coach, but we have a job on our administrative staff that aids the coaches. It's not coaching, but it will lead you down that road. What do you think?"

Well, I didn't have to. I sat on his old orange leather couch, burrito in hand, looked him in the eye and, like many high school recruits who had sat in the same seat, said, "I'm in."

Just like that I went from the Assistant Director of Football Relations to the note-taking, copy-making, stat-finding, number-crunching administrative assistant to the brainchildren Steve Sarkisian and Lane Kiffin. And I loved it. Oh, and I was wearing shorts and a t-shirt every day.

Life at USC was a daily adventure. With rockstars like Matt Leinart, Reggie Bush, the Song Girls and more—it was hard for it not to be. I had to pinch myself every time I walked out to Howard Jones Practice Field as a member of the University of Southern California football staff. This was USC football, the Los Angeles Memorial Coliseum, Rose Bowl titles, countless All-Americans and more. And here I was in the middle of it, a punk from PA.

Before every home game our team would go through the "Trojan Walk." This was a slow walk from our team buses outside the Coliseum to the 50-yard line, and over 10,000 fans would line up on each side of our squad, just reaching out to touch a player. The first time I experienced it was before our home opener against Arkansas—I walked from the bus to the Coliseum, down the 77 cement stairs to the field, around the bleachers to the student section and eventually to the 50-yard line. I said to myself, "From PA to LA, Yogi. You are living the dream."

I thought back to the countless times on New Year's Day when Glenn, Woody, Vince and I would turn on ABC to hear Keith Jackson describe the Trojans as they ran out of the tunnel in the hills of Pasadena, with legends like Ronnie Lott, Anthony Munoz, Sam "Bam" Cunningham, Pat Haden and Marv Goux watching from the sideline. With Dalton buried under three feet of snow, we would watch the sun-drenched warriors wearing the cardinal and gold compete on the gridiron. And now I was knee deep in this program—and loving every second of it.

My first year on the Trojan staff brought me two memories that remain as vivid as anything in my life—beating Notre Dame on the final drive of the game, and losing to Texas in the National Championship game on the final drive. But in each case it wasn't the actual game that I recall with such clarity—it was the locker room after one of the greatest victories in USC history and one of the worst losses.

At Notre Dame Stadium, in what is arguably one of the worst visiting locker rooms in the country, we sang our fight song, gave celebratory hugs and had grins from ear to ear, but what made the deepest impression on me happened when that excitement wound down. I took a long walk around the locker room, talked to offensive stars Matt Leinart, Reggie Bush, Dwayne Jarrett, and Ryan Kalil and found one common theme—our players knew they would win.

For sixty minutes they knew that they would come out on top. Down 31-28 with 2:02 remaining, they knew they would win. On fourth and nine, they believed in their preparation. And with seven seconds on the clock, they trusted that Matt would sneak in for the winning touchdown. But that "knowing" is something that was trained, not just innate in those great players. They were taken through a philosophy coined *Win Forever* by Coach Carroll.

At the heart of that approach is a simple yet bold vision, and one that made perfect sense to me: "do things better than they have ever been done before." With that came rules, uncompromising principles and beliefs that had become a part of our team's vernacular. We repeated them often: "Protect the team," "No whining, no complaining, no excuses," "It's all about the ball," "Everything counts," and "Respect everything." That simple vision and those beliefs kept our roster hungry and humble.

After understanding the program's vision, our players, all 105 of them, were crystal clear on the central theme of the program—competition. From keeping score in every drill or having a winner and loser each day in practice, a culture was formed at USC and it would walk with us into every locker room we visited.

The intensity of their commitment to *Win Forever* was what allowed this team to separate themselves from the pack. They understood that if they were confident in their ability and trusted in their preparation, they would be able to focus longer than their opponent, and that's exactly what happened on that October afternoon in South Bend. During the final drive of the game, our players were able to audible on fourth and nine to a pass play that changed the outcome. That confidence, trust and focus allowed Matt, Reggie, Dwayne, Ryan and everyone else to perform in the absence of fear and "know" they were going to win.

When we completed that 61-yard pass to Dwayne I was so jacked that I smashed my hand into the tv above my head and jumped up so fast my headphones got unplugged. But I was even more fired up that I was witnessing great players and a great team dedicate themselves to a philosophy uncommon not only in sports, but in overall performance.

The *Win Forever* philosophy instilled in our squad carried us to a 12-0 record and a berth in the National Championship game against the University of Texas, also undefeated. Rose Bowl, here we come.

This was as hyped a game as any in recent college football history as both California and Texas are hailed as the top two football states in the U.S.A. So while we were ready to put our all into the contest with the Longhorns, fans from L.A. and Austin were equally competitive. The air crackled with incredible intensity from all sides.

As a staff, we couldn't watch any more film. Our game plans were finalized and re-finalized, and every psychological ploy to gain an edge was exhausted by each member of the coaching staff. The only thing remaining was to play the game.

I walked onto the field on January 4, 2006, and an instant chill ran down my spine. With each step those chills would grow stronger. My eyes began to scan the crowd of 93,986 people, but it was as though I was peering into the stands in slow motion as I was able to see each individual's face clearly—the eyes, face paint, and growing anticipation. I paused at the 29-yard line to say hi to B.G., as I had done in our 12 previous games, and an inner smile and feeling of comfort came over me. My nerves relaxed, fear left me, and a sense of peace overcame all emotions. Our program had reached the goal we had set, and now we simply had to capture it. The Rose Bowl was the setting, an unprecedented third straight National Championship was at stake, and as I stood at the 29-yard line as a member of the USC staff, I knew that we belonged here. We had lived this experience, we owned this moment, and we were going to compete in a style like none other.

It was like a heavyweight bout with each team exchanging blows and responding in courageous fashion. The bright lights brought out the competitive nature in each player and the stars performed as expected. As the clock wound down and the game shortened, it seemed that whoever had possession of the ball last would be victorious. As luck would have it, the Longhorns regained the football with just over a minute to play and took their steps toward history, behind the magical play of Vince Young. When the clock struck :00, Texas had won 41-38.

So there I sat, high above the Rose Bowl in the press box, gazing across at the San Gabriel Mountains. The cool air was flowing through the open window, and I just breathed for a while, in and out. I couldn't even form a thought at first, much less speak. I looked at our staff—their faces blank, their eyes sunken. Time stood still for a few moments, and then I gathered my stuff and began the trek down those concrete stadium steps. As I walked past the empty beer bottles, over the spilled nacho holders, and onto the field of battle, a powerful thought came over me. I realized that yes, we lost and were disappointed, but also that our players had received a gift like none other.

I thought of my master's thesis, "What Makes a Great Coach Great" and how my study of Coach Carroll, Coach John Wooden and Coach Mike Krzyzewski revealed to me that each coach didn't just teach a philosophy to his players, they lived it too. The players at USC had learned an approach to life based on the central theme of Pete Carroll's life—competition—and while they came up a few inches short that night, they nonetheless were a part of something very special.

But to be honest, I couldn't help but wonder what Coach Carroll would say to the 105 young men and 15 or so members of our staff. I mean, any philosophy works when you win, but what now? What do you do after a loss? Is there a learnable moment? A silver lining?

So with each step down the Rose Bowl stairs, I gained speed. It was now a race to the locker room to hear what would be said. How would our head coach handle this loss, after 34 straight victories? How would those same players, who sat in Notre Dame's small locker room only months prior, speak after losing?

Just like he did that day as I sat on his old orange leather couch with a burrito, Coach Pete Carroll told the truth.

> *Men, we came within nineteen seconds of winning a third consecutive national title—nineteen seconds! To put in all of the work we put in, there is no way that nineteen seconds can define us as winners*

or losers. We've always said that for someone to beat us we either have to turn it over a number of times and give the game away or they have to play out of their minds, and tonight, number 10 had one of the greatest single game performances in the history of college football, and still, we were only nineteen seconds away from winning! Give Texas all the credit in the world, but you're still champions. Nineteen seconds will never define you.

The players—well, just like they did that day in South Bend after a dramatic win—also told the truth. Matt said it best: "I still think we're a better football team. They just made the plays in the end."

I understand how that could be seen as arrogant and disrespectful, but if you truly understand Coach Carroll's teachings, you would know that he teaches his players to not "hope" they will win, but "know" they will win. And to "know" that they are champions. Matt understood who won that night, but he also "knew" who the better team was.

That night I learned that Coach Carroll's *Win Forever* philosophy has nothing to do with winning. It has everything to do with maximizing on a daily basis who you are and who your team is. Texas did win that night in Pasadena. But we were still champions and the players and coaches who left our program after that season would take with them the philosophical clarity that wins or losses would not define the USC program and football tradition. Rather, what would define that legacy would be the moments that the journey to the Rose Bowl provided in 2006.

And for the record—I loved what Matt said. Remember, you show me a good loser and I'll show you a permanent one.

MACHU PICCHU

16

Let the world change you, and you can change the world.
– tagline for The Motorcycle Diaries

IT FELT LIKE MY HANGOVER LASTED A WEEK. On January 4, 2006, we had seen the National Championship taken from us, as Texas won the game in the final seconds. Moments later, the confetti was raining down over the Rose Bowl and the victorious Vince Young was being carried off the field by his fans. Google it and you'll see why I can't get the visual out of my mind, and why I had drowned my sorrows until the early hours of the morning.

The worst part for me, though, had been seeing our offensive line coach, Pat Ruel, in the locker room directly after the loss. Although he had been in the coaching profession for over 30 years, and had met Pete Carroll in 1977 when they both were graduate assistants at Arkansas, this was his first National Championship game. I couldn't help but think of what it would be like to have waited for some 30 years for this moment to come, and then to watch helplessly as it ran away from you on Vince Young's legs. It's a safe bet that his hangover was worse than mine.

Spring break arrived not a moment too soon. I needed to get away—to spend some time doing something other than football, which had been my 24/7 obsession since I arrived at USC. So I took inspiration from my favorite film, *The Motorcycle Diaries*, which I'd first seen in a run-down Brooklyn theater some years before. Ever since, I couldn't stop thinking about the life-defining journey it detailed, as two 20-something buddies tour South America on an ancient Norton 500, on a quest for fun, adventure, and women. But the particular aspect that kept coming back to me was the section of the film dedicated to the Inca Trail and Peru, and the profound insight that Che Guevara, on whose journals the film was based, had received there. So, like Che (except minus the beret), I set off for one the greatest wonders of the world, Machu Picchu, the Lost City of the Incas. At that point, I didn't know much about Che—I knew he believed that man's innate dignity was more important than boundaries of nations and race, and that he could change the world. That was all I had, but it was enough. I was sold on Machu Picchu and Che.

A calm came over me as soon as I boarded my flight to Peru: my traveling spirit had awakened. I began my exploration in Lima, a bustling melting pot on the Pacific. In short order, I met a gal who spoke no English, but we had a little chemistry, so, like any 23-year-old, I said hello, and by the end of the night said goodbye with a make-out session. Hey, I got to first base with a hot chick in Peru, so to me the trip was already a success. Is this what they mean by "language of the world"? Not enough that I'd read and re-read *The Alchemist*, Pablo Coehlo's irresistible book about shepherd boy Santiago, whose search for fortune becomes instead a journey to find the underlying theme to the life we lead, and the common language all cultures possess. I'd have to do further research, so off I went.

From the coastal desert and 21st century alpha city vibe of Lima, I headed high into the Andes, bound for ancient Cuzco, historical capitol of the Inca Empire, meeting people and absorbing various cultures along the way. The gateway to Machu Picchu, Cuzco is also a fascinating destination on its own, due to the engineering genius of its indigenous creators.

Centuries before the concept hit Western civilization, Cuzco was a planned city, and two rivers had been diverted to provide space for it. It is also a layered city—starting in the 1500's, colonial Spanish structures had been built on top of Inca buildings, which in turn rested on what the very first inhabitants had created. In a major earthquake in 1950, many of the Spanish era structures were destroyed, leaving the Inca underpinnings exposed and undamaged. The earlier, simpler building blocks of society had survived, whereas the later symbols of Spanish conquest had crumbled. There's a lesson in there somewhere, I think.

When it was time to begin the four-day trek along the Inca Trail, I instantly slipped into game mode. I'd been training for this hike, so the day of departure was actually game day in my mind. Only this game would last for four days, not four quarters.

The day started at 5:45 a.m. in wind and rain, with an ascent of 12,000 feet in front of us. Our climbing crew was from all over the world, and I bonded with two Aussies immediately. Cameron and Gavin were in their late 20s, and worked construction and random jobs back in Australia to make travel money. They'd explore the world, return home when the cash evaporated, and then head out again. I knew this jaunt would be a blast with those two mates on my team. The first day's trek was easy, even leisurely, as we walked through small Andean villages, with gorgeous vistas at every turn.

Good thing we conserved our strength, because day two we faced the climb to Dead Woman's Pass—the hardest leg of the journey. We hiked up a nearly vertical, skinny, winding path, dodging llamas sure-footedly bounding downhill. This, of course, increased the competition because my personal goal was to hike without stopping and get to the top quickly. Once there, I turned to look down at the mountain I had just scaled, and it took my breath away. My own feet had trod the same path that the early Quechuans had walked daily, and for that moment, on top of that mountain with my knees shaking uncontrollably, I felt like I was one of them. Clearly I had no clue what their society was like, but in my own head I was living the life they led, at least the physical part. The view was beyond awe-inspiring, but the most impressive aspect was when Cameron's 67-year-old father arrived at the top. Made me wish my own dad were there.

The third day was a little easier, physically at least, but much tougher on the emotions. As we hiked up and down through the rainforest and the various ruins, my imagination sprang to life. I felt like a kid again as I ran through the wet leaves, swung from the branches, and joked around with the group. That high ended abruptly when I rounded a bend into a remote village of three impoverished households, and spotted a young boy, maybe about 4 years old, sitting on a rock. I slowed to a walk as he looked at me, his deep, dark brown eyes expressionless. He was very quiet, almost too quiet for a 4-year-old, but I knew I saw a spark of life beneath that solemn stare. Even though his harsh surroundings offered him little hope, I was sure his short existence on this planet had not robbed him of his spirit. Or had it?

Instantly, I thought of Che and the journey that had transformed him from self-centered superficial kid to an adult who took responsibility for his fellow man. So I bent down, said hello to the little fella, spent a few minutes with him, and took his picture. Life is nothing without human contact—even if you don't share a language, you share the gift of life.

4:00 a.m. day four, we awoke to pouring rain. Our goal was to make it to what is called the "Sun Gate" by sunrise, so we slogged along the trail as fast as we could, and got there just in time. It was one of those sights that is forever imprinted in your brain—the sun rose to reveal our first spectacular glimpse of the fabled Lost City of the Incas in the distance. As my eyes gathered in the image, we walked closer and closer, and I remembered bits of history I'd learned about this great civilization. To have lived in this city in its prime, in the 15th and 16th centuries, must have been amazing—even now its construction is a feat of engineering that can't quite be explained. I explored the stone-lined stairs and paths for the next few hours, ending up at the sacred Intihuatana stone, which points directly at the sun during winter solstice. Such a peaceful and spiritually fulfilling city, I couldn't help but wonder what it must it have been like when news of Pizarro and the Spanish invading Cuzco reached these isolated mountain dwellers. They sent half their population to their deaths in that battle, and Cuzco was lost. The remaining inhabitants of Machu Picchu fled east to the even more remote Snow Mountains. And the city was frozen in time—the Spanish never found it, so its archeological treasures were never looted.

With no one left to tend to its manicured paths, Machu Picchu became nothing more than rock covered with grass, weeds, and trees, and remained that way until 1908 when a professor from Yale came across it. Thankfully, the National Geographic Society later had it restored by setting fire to half of the mountain to burn away underbrush and other vegetation. After a week of burning, a mystical city had emerged from the ashes.

The history of the Lost City made me think of similar stories that have come out of so many cultures worldwide that I had yet to learn about, and how much influence they have had on everyone on the planet. And at that moment I thought of my father's mom, Grammy Roth, who left one message imprinted on my mind when she passed away that spring: "Yogi, always keep learning."

So I leaned against a man-made wall thousands of years old and slowly slid my back down it. The minute I touched the cool stone, I let my imagination take over—I could hear the 2,000 Quechuans toiling away, I could sense their culture around me. And as I watched the wild llamas graze nearby, I, like Che in *Motorcycle Diaries*, felt completely in tune with the Lost City. Maybe it was the physical experience of hiking up the mountain, walking their ancient streets, and touching the stones they had carved—but I sensed a deep human bond with those who had lived here centuries before.

And I realized that the Lost City was never lost. We just couldn't see it.

THE DECISION

17

UPS AND DOWNS DEFINED MY SECOND SEASON as a member of the USC staff—the Lost City was a happy memory as I threw myself back into the world of the Trojans. Having just come off an appearance in the National Championship game, I finally had a clue what I was doing football-wise. So I entered the 2006 season feeling like a veteran. With a good understanding of L.A., too, I believed life couldn't get much better.

We had a young team and new quarterback, but were strong at wide receiver, the position I studied. Dwayne Jarrett and Steve Smith led the way with John David Booty at the helm. Although we began the season rolling, we hit a bump at Oregon State when we failed to convert on our final play. In the typical fashion of Pete Carroll-led teams, however, we came roaring back and were positioned to go to the National Championship game for the third consecutive year if we could beat arch-rival UCLA in our final game of the regular season.

And we laid an egg. For whatever reason, we lost that afternoon in a game that we should have dominated.

The picture is vivid: as the clock faded to zero, UCLA fans flooded the floor of the Rose Bowl with confetti, just as Texas fans had done only 11 months earlier. I sat in the same seat in the press box, my face in my hands, and an expression that said, "What just happened?"

The second-worst weeklong hangover of my life commenced.

Then came my unforgettable welcome to the chaotic world of the coaching profession. First, Steve Sarkisian, who was interviewing for the Oakland Raiders' head coaching job, asked me to come aboard to help coach the receivers if he got the job. Obviously jacked to think of coaching at the NFL level, I said, "Hell, yeah!"

Three weeks later, Sark was finally offered the job. Just as I was about to congratulate him on becoming the youngest head coach in the NFL, he turned the position down to remain at USC. A shock to the sports world and a shock to me. I said to myself, "Wow, this is a wild profession."

So I was set to return to USC for a third season. Well, until a few hours later, when circumstances changed again. Lane Kiffin, our offensive coordinator and the staff member with whom I worked the most closely, had impressed Al Davis of the Raiders so much that Al actually offered him the head coaching job after Sark said no thanks.

Now imagine for a second being a 25-year-old graduate assistant. One day I'm going to the Raiders, the next I exhale and accept that I'll stay at USC, and the following day I'm offered a gig, once again, with the Raiders. It was awesome!

After Coach Carroll helped me decide that going to Oakland might be best, I accepted the job. And for the next week I celebrated like a rockstar because I was going to the league. Thanks, perhaps, to me playing the NFL card, I met more cool ladies that week than I did in the previous two years, and my ego soared.

Then a call from Coach Carroll came at 2:12 a.m. on a Friday night. "Yogi, I think we might have something for you."

"What, Coach? Are you serious?"

"I'll pick you up in the morning. Let's grab some breakfast."

So we went to breakfast, and he offered me the assistant quarterbacks job, working with Sark. The organizing of film, stapling of practice scripts, and mundane, miserable responsibilities would no longer be part of my job description; instead, I would be teaching, coaching, and learning.

What a dilemma. I had a great opportunity to get to the NFL at a young age, and another opportunity to work with Heisman-worthy quarterbacks at USC. Both equally exciting jobs, one in Oakland, and the other in Los Angeles. But pick one, and I'd lose the other.

I was still leaning toward northern California and the NFL. I had worked side-by-side with Coach Kiffin, and he was one of my closest confidants. I wanted to help him succeed and find out if my coaching philosophies could work at the highest level while learning about the NFL.

With two offers and a deadline… as well as about a million "expert" opinions on what I should do, I needed some time alone. Evidently, I needed to put my Australian-born theory to the test. Life is simple and I had a simple decision—stay or leave. But I had made it complex by gathering as much information as possible. Now, coming full circle, I needed to get back to the simplicity of the question: stay or leave?

Everyone told me the same thing: "Trust your gut." I'd look at my stomach and say, "Come on now, talk to me." It would say, "Go to the Raiders," and I'd say, "That feels pretty good." I'd ask again and it would say, "Stay at USC," and I'd say, "That feels pretty good, too."

Clearly the gut was giving very confusing advice. So one particular day, as the clock was ticking down, I walked out onto the beach, sat on top of a big sand dune with my journal, and made a very ordinary pro and con list. Which again was no help. But after thinking long and hard (and surfing for hours on end), I realized I had come face to face with what I wanted in life and who I was at the time. I looked up the coast and could see Malibu, and looked down the coast to the magnificent Palos Verdes Peninsula. And ultimately, I recognized that I wanted to enter the NFL only because it was the NFL. Not because I wanted to learn the West Coast offense, or because I wished to see what the draft process is like, and surely not because I wanted to live in Oakland.

I called my Dad one last time and just listened to him. "Son, at the end of the day a resumé is just a piece of paper. So make this decision with your heart, but understand that you cannot make a decision based on prestige, as that will wear off. Just be true to yourself and you'll be a happy man."

And that is when I stood up from the sand in Hermosa Beach, opened my cell phone, looked out to the Pacific Ocean and the set of waves rolling in, and called Lane Kiffin to say thank you, but no thanks.

I would stay in L.A.

SARK AND WIN FOREVER

18

Your preparation will set you free. – *Coach Steve Sarkisian*

"I'M SO JACKED! I'M SO FREAKIN' JACKED!" was on my voicemail. As if it was from Jessica Alba, I saved it on my beat-up mobile phone for over two years. While I never played it for friends, I would stumble upon it when checking voicemails, but would never delete it.

The problem was that it wasn't from Jessica Alba—we had yet to meet. Hence the "as if…" Rather, it was from Coach Steve Sarkisian. Not that I confuse him with Jessica Alba. It's just that, oh, never mind.

After I turned down the Oakland Raiders offer to become USC's Assistant Quarterbacks coach, Sark was the first one to call me. On a recruiting trip, he was snowed in at the Springdale, Arkansas airport, and left me that message that I saved the entire time I was at USC. Sark and I would now work side by side—he was the Assistant Head Coach/Offensive Coordinator/Quarterbacks coach, and I would be his assistant.

Two days later, Sark made his way back to L.A. and the training was on. He played the role of Mr. Miyagi and I was Daniel-san. Okay, not exactly, but Sark and I would meet in his office every morning at 7:00 a.m. He'd have his venti Starbucks and I'd have my white notepad, rapidly writing down every word that came out of his mouth, whether or not I understood any of it. It didn't matter—I had never been happier or more excited. I was learning about the position I had always dreamt of playing back in PA—quarterback. And I was learning it from a master.

Sark's words eventually began to make sense as he taught me everything from how to properly take a snap from center, how to find a rhythm in one's cadence, and how to dissect a defense. And once he explained that, we began to discuss how an offense attacks a defense and how defensive coordinators game plan offenses. And lastly, Sark taught me how to trust my instinct on game day.

He had a way with teaching—he made it easy, broke it down like my Dad had when I was on the verge of failing 8th grade earth science. Sark taught me how to play quarterback, how to speak quarterback, and how to teach quarterback. And he did it in a fashion that was fun, exciting, and entertaining. Before we knew it, training camp was over and it was time for our first game against Idaho.

As I slowly jogged onto the floor of the Los Angeles Memorial Coliseum, I took a moment to gaze at the bright lights, the cardinal and gold, and the 92,500 screaming fans. Then I took another moment to appreciate how fortunate I was. This was different from Pitt, and this was many miles and years from Lackawanna Trail. This was USC: 150 plus All-Americans, seven Heisman Trophy winners, eleven National titles, Traveler, the two-finger "V" salute, and the world-famous Song Girls. All this and more in a huge city with no professional team, and there I stood—an official coach. Sure, I was a graduate assistant, but nonetheless, I was coaching ball and loving every moment.

"This big enough for ya, Yogs?" Sark would bark over the headset before kick-off. I looked back, smiled, and in a blink the season was over. Sark had called the plays and I had signaled them to our quarterback. As each game plan came and went, many lessons were taught, and in twelve short months I went from having a GED in quarterback play to earning a master's degree from Quarterback U and Professor Sark. But like a college degree, it had little to do with an actual diploma and everything to do with the journey Sark and I went on that year in Heritage Hall and on the field.

I'd been learning from him for two seasons, so we had a solid foundation, and we were already close friends. But working together for literally 18 hours a day, we got to know each other far beyond the game. I'd bring up mundane, and probably lame, 26-year old questions about QBs and life; he talked about his career plans, why he turned down the Raiders, his incredible family and everything in between. I'd show up at his house on random off-days to hang out, barbeque and have a few laughs. He'd meet me at the beach for lunch, a surf or to toss the pigskin around. We could talk about anything. Never really sure if I wanted to become a "lifer," Sark not only accepted that, he understood it—and we would actually talk openly about it. We went from teacher and pupil to family—he a big brother to me, and I a younger brother to him.

During that memorable season, I also learned what it meant to *Win Forever*. At first glance, winning forever means that you win all of your games, win national championships, get articles written about you, and reign in the world of college football. But another look shows that winning forever has little to do with any of that.

Marching through our season, we had already racked up two major losses (to Stanford and Oregon). Although both killed our momentum and kept us out of the national title picture, both also provided us with a means to prove who we were.

We did just that. While taking our lumps from the press and the fans, we came together by rededicating ourselves to the Trojan motto, "Fight On." We competed to be the best team we could possibly be by controlling what was directly in front of us, and never allowed the disappointment of losing to diminish the mentality and energy we needed on the practice field every day. We would maximize our potential by competing relentlessly every day. That's the ultimate meaning of *Win Forever*.

When the season ended with us burying Illinois 49-17, setting a Rose Bowl record for most total yards and most points scored, I was thrilled with a championship, a record sixth straight Pac-10 title for Coach Carroll, a record sixth straight BCS bowl game, a record sixth straight top-5 finish, and another undefeated November. It was a rewarding season on many levels and one that would catapult our staff and our players into 2008 with a laser-like focus.

Then the off-season came and the coaching carousel began anew. Sark had multiple offers, as he was now one of the hottest young coordinators in the country, and I too looked at a few jobs. Most graduate assistants would jump at any chance to get a full-time gig, but I knew what I was learning would separate me from the pack if and when I chose to leave. And I still wasn't ready—there was more to learn and who better to learn from than one of my closest friends?

So Sark and I did what we had been doing for over a year with a new goal—we began the pursuit of the coveted Ph.D in quarterback play while never wavering from Professor Sark's motto, "Your preparation will set you free."

And just like that—at 7:00 a.m. in Sark's office we sat—he with a venti Starbucks, me with a white notepad, preparing for my fourth season with the USC Trojans.

Both of us "jacked." Obviously.

THE HESPERUS

19

Time on my brow has set his seal... – William Roth, on April 22, 1859

THE EDGE OF THE EARTH had been on my mind since I was 8 years old. I'd read about it in my great-great-great grandfather's journal, *The Hesperus*, which sat on my bedside table. In those transcribed pages were stories about how he, at 25, jobless and on the brink of disaster, had abruptly left New York City for Boston Harbor. His future, once so full of promise, now offered him but one choice—to make his life on the high seas.

He called the ship Hesperus home for the next 387 days as he set out from Boston to the southernmost tip of South America and ultimately San Francisco. His journal detailed how he sailed through treacherous storms, facing death squarely between the eyes and developing a work ethic and life philosophy along the way.

I would read those stories by flashlight under my sheets when I was a kid, and I'd visualize what the Falkland Islands looked like or how rough the seas were. But what truly piqued my interest was the way my great-great-great grandfather became immersed in other cultures around the world. In particular, I was fascinated with what's called the edge of the earth, popularly known as Cape Horn.

After three seasons working for the Trojans, the urge to see that part of the world for myself had never felt stronger. After a quick visit to Kayak.com, I figured out my flight plan, booked it, and was on my way to Santiago, Chile. From there I'd would make my way south, with a stop in the Patagonia region for some camping before arriving in the small port town called Puerto Williams, the southernmost inhabited town in South America. On the border of Argentina, it is where the sailors of my great-great-great grandfather's day made their final stop before attempting to round Cape Horn.

During my past travels, I had learned that although the initial goal is always to see various sights or to absorb various cultures, in reality what you see and hear most of all is yourself. And from the very start of this trip, I knew I was on some sort of personal quest.

I landed in Santiago without knowing a word of Spanish, but let my thumb do the talking for me as I hitched a ride to a nearby hostel. I quickly realized that not many people in the capital of Chile speak English. Somehow, though, I managed to stumble into one person that did. Well, sort of. Gioninna was her name, a 5'7" stunning brunette with elegant features and a beautiful smile. Her English was pretty minimal, but our non-verbal communication was excellent as we wandered throughout the city, laughing and chatting. At some point, that voice inside me chimed in, "I think I just fell in love."

After a night on the town that included local food, museums, and lessons on the history of Santiago, I headed south for the Patagonia region and Torres del Paine, the national park that protects the spectacular mountains, glaciers, and lakes of southern Chile.

I flew into Punta Arenas, a decent-sized city on the Strait of Magellan, then hopped on a bus to a tiny town 200 miles north on the edge of Torres del Paine. The first thing I noticed was the silence—it was breathtakingly quiet. Where was that hum of modern life that we're so used to? I heard the sounds of nature, the steady Patagonian wind, but not much else. It was desolate, almost eerie, with nothing around that I recognized as part of my life. Just this tiny outpost, with only a few homes.

I easily found the town's hostel—which was a room rented out from a local family. Then the next morning I went on a day tour of glaciers, waterfalls, and other local sights—the only time on this trip that I was actually with a group. The magnificence of the scenery reduced us to silence, though—in particular the sight of Lago Grey. An enormous mountain lake surrounded by black rocks and sand, it is being taken over by massive glaciers pushing their way out into the frigid water. If you listen carefully, you can hear the sound of the ice moving as it twists its way down the slope. Standing above this are the three soaring towers of Torres del Paine, never for a moment letting you forget who the mother of this vast and awe-inspiring park is.

I ditched the group at the end of the day and camped out in the wilderness, while they sought the comfort of the little village a few miles away. As soon as it got dark, a freezing rain began to fall—and I was very grateful for my miserable little tent, although I wasn't sure it would protect me from the herd of wild horses that called this campground home. As a matter of fact it wasn't even protecting me from the wind, which was growing steadily stronger.

But it was cool. Nothing would stop me from waking up at 5:00 a.m. to make it to the three peaks and back before the afternoon bus trip. With less than a 45-minute mid-morning window where one can see the three towers before the fog grows thick and hides Torres del Paine, I knew I would be in a race against the sun. Sleep was not an option: the thundering hoofs just feet from my head kept me awake most of the night. So I lay there, writing in my journal until it was time for departure. I set off on schedule, with the aid of my trusty flashlight (okay, not so trusty—the batteries seemed to be growing weaker with each step I took) and fairly general directions from a park ranger. "Head north, and cross two bridges" was his helpful advice.

Alone, cold, shrouded in darkness, I began my trek with nature, the stars, and the wind gods acting as my compass. The only thing I could do was trust my instincts. With all five senses alive and all ten fingers freezing, I made my way to bridge #1. A huge moment: now I knew I was headed in the right direction. When I came upon bridge #2, I was on cloud nine.

Euphoria quickly vanished. I could see nothing, but was using my video camera to document what was happening, or at least what I thought was happening. I could hear the water crashing violently below, but I couldn't tell how high I was. My feet told me I was on a footbridge of unknown length; my left hand told me there was one railing, while my right hand was busy with the now nearly useless flashlight.

I moved carefully, feeling my way forward, bracing myself against the relentless winds. High up on a swaying footbridge in the pitch-black Patagonia darkness, I decided it might be time for some self-reflection, some mental notes for my next excursion. If there ever was one.

My extensive preparation for the trip had been relatively off the cuff, I admit. While I did some *Lonely Planet* research, I must have skimmed over the part that read, "high-quality foul-weather gear is essential; a warm synthetic sleeping bag and wind-resistant tent are imperative," as I had no hat, and just a light windbreaker to keep me warm and dry. Which failed, since I was now freezing and soaked to the bone. Nature was Winning Forever and I was cold.

Just then, I felt something shift beneath my feet. A subtle shift, nothing dangerous—the angle of the bridge had changed. I was past the midpoint. And the winds stopped. My tension evaporated, and I became comfortable there high above the thundering river. I could sense, though still not see, that on the left, the sun would rise, and on the right, a massive mountain loomed.

The second I reached the other side, the race was on. I sprinted to the first bend of the switchback trail up the mountain, where I caught the first rays of sunshine. I whipped out my camera, pressed REC—and nothing happened. No juice. Not even a warning light. I switched the batteries around, and even licked the tip of each one. Is that a myth or does it work? It didn't for me, and disappointed doesn't cover it—I was pretty damned angry and even began to yell at the Sony Camcorder as if it were a freshman quarterback who wasn't avoiding a rush in the pocket. But that inner voice that so often says, "Suck it up," said exactly that. So I did.

As I continued to climb, the path got narrower and steeper. The moon slid lower in the sky, while the sun almost reluctantly revealed his face. A passage from my great-great-great grandfather's journal popped into my mind and said it best: "This far south the sun nor sets or rises, rather appears and says good evening."

I rounded a pass, and suddenly the mountains of Patagonia lay before me, clear and snowcapped, and the lakes below caught the first beam of sunlight and shone radiant blue and green. Nature seemed to change her colors every few minutes here, much like Uluru—but I was alone. No dramatic speeches captured on video, no Jerome from Boston. Just me. Solo. I stood still for a moment, and let the sights and sounds of Chile wash over me.

Two and a half hours after I had started, I reached the first campsite. It's typically an hour trek, maybe an hour fifteen if you're slow. Those cautious steps on the wobbly footbridge had slowed me down more than I had realized, and now I faced a time crunch. I had a choice to make: do I push toward Torres del Paine or head back to catch the bus? I chose to push forward, as I had come too far not to get a glimpse of the three towers of Patagonia.

So the competition began. I ran, jumped, and scrambled my way to the next pass. Hurtling through thick forests and jungle-like vegetation and leaping over streams and logs, I recaptured the early euphoria of the day. By 9:40 a.m. I stood at the base of the final stage—a nearly vertical climb to the top of the trail, the closest point to the granite spires that give the park its name.

Four hikers were coming down from the top, and warned me that not only were the boulders slick and dangerous, but that the fog was rolling in and would be far too dense by the time I made it up the rocky slope to see the Torres del Paine. But I had to go. If my great-great-great grandfather could survive the perilous waters of Cape Horn a few hundred miles to the south, then I could make it up these last few hundred feet.

Let me tell you, USC strength and conditioning coach Chris Carlisle's stair climbing routine was a snap compared to this difficult path. I clawed my way up boulders, hurdled rocks and jumped over streams. Inspired to reach the top, I hit the "zone," that state of peak performance when mind and body are effortlessly in tune.

And then, there I was. I stood on a boulder five times my size, gazing at the astonishing natural beauty spread out before me. Two of the three Torres were visible; only one was obscured by fog. And below them lay a sparkling olive green lake. I sat on the massive rock, let out a long exhale, and grinned as sweat dripped down my face and steam rose from my head. The fifth person to get to the top of the Torres del Paine that morning, I celebrated my feat by just sitting and staring.

I wanted to write in my journal, but I couldn't find my pen. Almost by design, I'd lost it somewhere on the trail. So I just relaxed, deep in thought, proud of my accomplishment, but with a profound sense of humility and respect for this grand national park. Birds swooped and soared above me, and animals went about their daily routine around the lake below as I drank in the crisp cool air, the purest I had ever breathed. I guess it was nature's turn to write a journal entry: "This. Is. Living."

Just on the off-chance that my camera had somehow come back to life, I took it out of my backpack and started fiddling with it. Suddenly and completely inexplicably, it powered on. I quickly aimed it at the Torres del Paine, adjusted my framing, and watched in awe as the fog miraculously lifted to show the third and final tower. If any of us have ever seen photographs of Chile, this is the image that we all have imprinted in our brains: those three starkly graceful stone spires stretching toward the deep blue sky, lit by a low-angled sun, and dominating the surrounding landscape by sheer elegance.

Thirty seconds later my camera died again, and I had zero desire to attempt resuscitation. I just sat there, silent and at peace—feeling just as I had when Pitt beat Notre Dame, or when USC took on Texas in the national title game.

But there was no time for reflection. I knew I had to be back at base camp to catch the only bus into town, so with it now 10:30, I was racing the clock. It was 45 minutes down the rocks, almost straight down. I jumped, I slid, and had a blast—if anyone had seen me, they'd have thought I was 12 years old, or that I'd just made out with the princess of Torres del Paine.

Back to reality: it was now 11:15. I knew I had to make up time, so I began to sprint through the woods and jungle. I told myself I was being chased by hostile Patagonian rebels, and this little fantasy brought me to the next pass in 45 minutes, beating the standard time by a good 15 minutes.

And now I'd arrived at the final leg back to camp, the one that had been my greatest challenge on the trip up. It was by far the longest section, but a renewed spirit gave my legs the strength to pump as if I were training for football camp back at Pitt. I ran with a passion, and even managed to take some pictures, say good morning to other hikers, and even talk with two Israeli soldiers who had just finished their tour of duty.

Finally, as I caromed down to base camp just before the bus left, I bumped into two cute Belgian women, and was thrust back into society with these two foreign blonds as my guides. Decent timing, I must say.

Exhausted but exhilarated, I thought I'd catch a little shut-eye on the ride down to Punta Arenas before my flight out the next morning. Instead, as my body thawed out, I furtively glanced at the Jessica Alba look-alike behind me, sitting with a complete clown. Why is it that the hotter the girl, the dorkier the guy? Another deep life question left unanswered in the South

American wilderness.

The kid directly across from me had a more productive idea: he was reading *Into the Wild,* and kept smiling and chuckling as if he were trekking in Canada alongside Christopher Johnson McCandless, the real-life hero of the book. So I dug through my backpack for *The Hesperus*—entertaining for me, though Jessica Alba remained oblivious.

The bus pulled into Punta Arenas at 10:00 p.m., and I stepped out onto the sidewalk to meet the wind, rain, and chill that I thought I had left behind in the Patagonian Mountains. Unsure of where to spend the night, I started chatting with the reader who had sat across from me, and he offered me his map. His name was Braden, and for six months he had explored Peru, Chile, and Easter Island, making ends meet by sleeping on trains and working in run-down towns along the way. In Easter Island, after he had met a girl, his planned two-week vacation had turned into an eighty-two day relocation and love story.

That night, Braden and I found the town's cheapest hostel to crash in, but I couldn't sleep: my body was still defrosting from my trek, and this particular establishment had no heat. The other guests there—young and old, from all over the world—were fascinating: a European couple traveling in a beat-up Volkswagen bug that leaked in the rain; two French brothers exploring the Chilean countryside (I think one of them had a crush on me); a nomadic teacher from London recounting the same story over and over again; a student from New York City studying abroad; and the crazed hostel owner we called Mama.

Mama constantly screamed at the European couple to stop talking, but with a few bottles of Chilean wine empty on the table, her requests went unheeded as they yelled back in jumbled Spanish. The two brothers sang Queen's "Mama, I've Just Begun" in thick French accents, the teacher kept chuckling and filling his wine glass, the student lay on the couch curled up in her blanket reading a novel, Braden was looking at images of his Easter Island girlfriend on his Facebook page, and I sat by the stove as, one by one, each toe regained feeling.

From Punta Arenas, I caught my flight to Puerto Williams, which was the whole point of this journey. The southernmost inhabited city in South America, and once one of the most influential ports in the world, it is smaller than Dalton. When Magellan discovered the strait to the north which now bears his name, many sailors opted for the shortcut and cut Puerto Williams off their itinerary. And for nearly a century, since the opening of the Panama Canal, the town has been in a valiant struggle for survival—now it serves only those hardy few who take the true long way around the continent, as well as those headed for scientific explorations in Antarctica. It's a town that needs a chance—and it reminded me of Dalton, in some weird way. They had no football team, but they did have pride, passion and an energy that was bottled up. They just needed an outlet—yes, the edge of the earth needed a voice—so I began the search to find it.

It was freezing as I walked around, exploring the sailboats, the naval shipyard, and extremely run-down pockets of town. I recalled from my great-great-great grandfather's journal that he passed through this town—but what was he thinking in 1858? This would have been the last place he had felt earth beneath his feet before rounding the Horn.

The latitude and longitude alone would make any man of the seas second-guess sailing the nearby treacherous waters, to say nothing of the unpredictable and harsh weather. Also, the nickname "Sailors' Graveyard" might give a guy second thoughts. My great-great-great grandfather's description of the relentless storms that whip the seas has gripped my imagination since I was a little boy—maybe it was their personification as Old Boreas, the Greek god of the winter wind, that got to me:

> *Monday, February 1, 1859*
>
> *This is another eventful day on our passage. Old Boreas never showed himself more violent than today, save once on the other side of the land. All the rest of the passage he was asleep until we arrived off Cape Horn, when he woke up for about three weeks and then again went to sleep until this morning, when he came down upon us with a vengeance for about twenty minutes, ripping and tearing our sails at a fearful rate. He took us unawares. We had all sails set and were going along at about ten knots an hour with the yards nearly square when a squall arose. It did not seem threatening so we took in no sail until it was right upon us. In thirty minutes we were under close reef topsails but we never got the sails in until the squall was over. So*

we made sail again and at 12 o'clock our latitude was 33.30, with
liberty almost within our grasp. I hope nothing will happen to snatch
it from us.

But none of this deterred him. My bedside companion had a plan, an
agenda, something he needed to accomplish. Much like I did.

Lonely Planet had recommended a local hostel, but even though this home
was warm and cozy, something didn't feel right. I was being pulled in another
direction, to a hostel that was run by a 79-year-old man named Ben and his
wife, a local woman. A lifelong sailor who had circumnavigated the world
countless times, Ben had witnessed life at levels I cannot even fathom, much
like my great-great-great grandfather.

For three days I would wake up and explore this vast and dreary land,
searching for the ingredients that would bring it back to life. And then each
night I would go upstairs to Ben's home and talk to his two daughters and his
wife, who was about to set sail around the Cape for herself. Finally, my final
night, I asked Ben if he and I could chat for a few minutes. He obliged and
led me to his office with a subtle move of his finger.

I sat down and felt two hours go by as if it were two minutes. Ben recounted a few of his adventures, discussed his life choices and chatted about
Puerto Williams. But when I brought up *The Hesperus* and my great-great-
great grandfather, he immediately perked up and became much more interested in what I had to say, as if a respect had been forged. It was similar to the
power of bloodlines in football recruiting—if a player is the son of a coach,
he is instantly lifted to a higher status, part of a select group.

I looked out at the moon shining through the window that overlooked the
edge of the earth, and asked him one final question, "Ben, is someone born
to sail around Cape Horn?"

He leaned forward in his chair, peered at Argentina to the east, and then
back at the magnificent and rough seas that he respected profoundly.

"Yogi," he said, laying out the challenge, "you were born to sail around
Cabo de Hornos."

But not on this journey—it was fast coming to a close. My final day in
Chile brought me back to Santiago, where my trip had begun seemingly
months earlier. I reunited with Gioninna, and she and I roamed the streets of

the city as we had before, but with one important difference: we could now communicate with actual language. After eight days in Chile, I was making a linguistic comeback on par with the Red Sox's performance when they beat my beloved Yankees in 2004. Español, baby. Smooth, very smooth.

Though we failed to exchange vows that day, we did allow ourselves to become close in a way that sometimes only strangers can, and I can officially say that we were boyfriend and girlfriend, if only for one day. Arm in arm, we walked, ate, and romanced through Santiago's version of Central Park, sharing ice cream and making out like long-lost lovers John Cusack and Kate Beckinsdale in *Serendipity*.

But as we neared the street which would mark the end of our time together, each step got slower, and each kiss became longer. As our feet crossed that imaginary line back into reality, we were neither sad nor upset. We knew that two lives had been changed by the hours we spent together; two cultures were intertwined and two people meshed.

Now I know you may be thinking, "No kidding. Yogi, you just made out with a beautiful Chilean gal you'll never see again—let us know when you come back to the real world," but that's not entirely fair. This trip confirmed for me that life is to be lived, life is about learning, and life is love… and all we need to do is really listen and be open to it.

In Santiago de Chile, Patagonia, Cabo de Hornos and back, it didn't matter the language spoken, the path run, or the boat sailed—it was about the journey, maximizing the fun, embracing the challenge, and diving head first into the many opportunities for self-exploration that traveling brings.

As my great-great-great grandfather wrote on April 22, 1859, which happened to be Good Friday and his 26th birthday, "Time on my brow has set his seal, and I start to find myself a man."

As I flew back from Chile to L.A., also 26, I leaned back in my seat, looked in my small leather-bound journal and smiled—I could not have agreed more.

SACRAMENTO AND POLK

20

IN DALTON OR IN HERMOSA BEACH I always felt that I could listen to my friends, my family, and the players I coached. But after my journey to the edge of the earth, I discovered that I could listen to myself in a way I never had before—I was clearer and more focused about what mattered to me. Sports are all about passion and emotion—sometimes you forget that exists in real life as well.

And that's how I found myself on the corner of Sacramento and Polk in San Francisco, on the verge of a heart-to-heart with my high school girlfriend. I'd thought about her often in the years following our parting, and had even seen her a couple of times. There was something unfinished between us. Or was there? I had to find out—and time was not on my side. She was making plans, and they didn't include me.

I'd had the epiphany 30,000 feet above the earth, on the plane back to L.A. So at my earliest opportunity, I flew up to San Francisco. Coach Carroll's best friend, Dave Perron, had set up a meeting for me with a friend of his who worked with the Oakland A's—so technically I was there on business, even though it didn't look like it. The only car available from Enterprise was a white Sebring convertible, so I had to follow my convertible rule—top down unless it's freezing. It was May in the Bay Area, so it was relatively tolerable. Plus, frankly, the ride was sweet.

You know how you compare big emotional moments in your life to what you've seen in the movies? Maybe it's just a way to keep the feelings at a distance, or maybe it's a way to give them the drama they deserve. The buildup, in my mind, was intense—it'd look great on film, all passionate, man on a mission, etc. All that remained was for the drama to play itself out.

We've seen the opening shot—white convertible crossing the Bay Bridge. Now we would move to Ghirardelli Square, an iconic site for the set-up. When I first saw her, I must admit a little something came over me. Not sure what it was, maybe the power of that first love? If you were watching on the big screen, you'd read my physical reaction, even in a long shot, and then the director would zoom in for a closeup, where you'd see our eyes meet, and then our quick embrace. Nothing too serious, but definitely some raw emotion.

We walked around the city, enjoying each other's company, almost as if we were on a date. We got ice cream, we chatted and laughed, and we recounted life lessons learned in Dalton. While sitting on a stoop overlooking the Pacific, we talked about the people we used to know, and the life we'd led back in PA. Along the boardwalk, we moved on to our families, personal issues, and careers. Two-thirds of the day was borderline b.s. for people who understood each other the way we did, and we both knew it. The tension was building, ever so subtly; we were avoiding the confrontation.

I could feel what was happening—she was slipping further and further away, and there was nothing I could do. As we walked up hilly Polk Street to her apartment, I finally brought up the topic.

I asked her if she was ready for what she was about to do and her response was not what I expected. Now I wasn't imagining that she didn't love her life; I think she was completely enthralled by it. But I was questioning whether her life was what she had pictured, what she had always dreamt of. I had so much on the tip of my tongue, and she knew it. The big dramatic moment was right in front of us, like a giant boulder on a mountain, but I wouldn't touch it. I didn't want to. Truth be told, I was ready to tell her not to follow through, ready to tell her that the timing wasn't right, ready to tell her that she wasn't ready... ready to tell her I still loved her. But instead of talking, I just listened.

Yet not just to her. As in Chile, I listened to my heart.

As we reached the top of Polk, I, for the first time, felt at peace about her. I stopped, turned to face the Pacific, which served as the backdrop for our final scene. Then I turned back to her, and, in our film, the camera would again zoom in to capture the words unsaid, the thoughts unspoken. I gazed back at the nearly vertical street we had trekked together, and then at the ocean beyond. I took a deep breath, and then another and another, as she talked and I listened. I was still at peace—still no impulse to make my move. I guess I knew my role and knew my lines for our final act, and understood what I had to do—or not do. There was no lustful kiss, no Jerry Maguire-esque speech, not even a verbal response from me.

My heart just opened up and I smiled. I gave her a hug, and as though we were synchronized soulmates for one more moment, she and I grasped onto each other's shoulder blades a little bit tighter. We smelled each other's fragrances a little bit longer. And we looked into each other's eyes a little bit deeper.

On that corner of Sacramento and Polk, I listened to my heart and said good-bye. She did too. And for the final time, by look and touch alone, we expressed those three little words that had meant so much to us so long ago.

And then I turned and walked away.

Strolling toward the Pacific, I didn't look back, didn't wonder what if, and didn't have a single regret. I just let her go. After ten years, I let her go.

Fade out.

THE LANGUAGE OF PEACE

21

SIX WEEKS LATER, SOLDIERS WITH UZIS surrounded me. I had just hopped off the El-Al flight to Israel, and security at Ben-Gurion Airport was even tighter than usual, due to negotiations between the Palestinians and the Israelis about a prisoner exchange.

It was my birthright tour—Jewish charities and the Israeli government offer an all-expenses-paid trip to Jews ages 18 to 26 who've never visited Israel, and my free ticket was about to expire. In return, I knew that those who fund this program hope to influence young Jews and educate them on their homeland, impress upon them the importance of their heritage, and stress the significance of Jewish marriage and Jewish family. Although my birthright trip would be a ten-day tour of the entire country as a part of a crew of thirty young adults, I added five days. Group travel isn't my style—I'm more of a solo guy and wanted time on the back end for myself.

The first sign that this trip would be momentous came immediately, when I took my seat on the plane next to Rachel, 79, from Poland. She was the spitting image of Baba—not just the way she looked, but also, eerily, the way she spoke. It was her sense of humor, though, that touched me the most. She had a beautiful laugh, coupled with a warm heart. It was as if both Baba and my mom were sitting there next to me.

And then my first night in Israel I roomed with two guys, Tommy and Morris. Ironically, Morris is also the name of my grandfather, Baba's husband. Coincidence—or extreme version of right place and right time? I really felt I was meant to be doing exactly what I was doing.

Morning one brought a huge Israeli breakfast (plenty of fresh fruit and vegetables grown on local kibbutzim) and a long and impassioned talk from the program's president, Momo. He spoke of what it meant to be Jewish and what it meant to carry on our heritage—and then he moved on to the power of love, how one cannot be afraid of love, and how we could find it here. We also met our tour guide, Reut—picture Angelina Jolie in Israeli army gear. As a thoroughly trained soldier, she was an expert on the history of the Middle East and knew her country inside and out, in addition to being extremely attractive. We were in competent hands.

Our first stop was Haifa, the town where Mom was born and spent her first years. An ancient and picturesque port city in northern Israel, it sits on the Mediterranean. It took me a while to visualize this bustling business center as a small city full of kibbutzniks that it was fifty years earlier when my mom was a child.

From there, we went east into the mountains to Tzfat, one of Israel's most revered spiritual centers, and the place where Kabbalah, Jewish mysticism, had flourished centuries before. We walked the cobbled streets, and then sat down with a man who has spent his life learning about the Kabbalah and the art associated with it. He spoke of the power of positive thinking, the law of attraction, the concept of expecting something great to happen, and the importance of developing an overall philosophy.

Most significantly, he spoke of the power behind one's name. As I sat in the summer heat in a small mountainside town in the heart of Israel, I learned that Zohar, my middle name and also an extremely popular name in Israel, has a deep history in Judaism. It refers to a collection of commentaries on the Torah, and is intended to guide those who already have a deep spiritual understanding of their souls. In its many discussions, it deals with the nature of the divine and man, and suggests that the grace of heaven springs directly from the justness and innate morality of man. In its most basic form, the Zohar is a guide to life—a way to bring spirituality into everyday existence.

But what practically knocked me out wasn't anything the man said. Instead, it was the painting hanging behind him—a blue star with various symbols drawn within it. Slowly, without a word, I stepped closer as I blinked tears from my eyes.

What I saw there was an image that has transfixed me since I drew it in fifth grade. I don't know when I first saw it, but it made its mark on my subconscious somewhere along the way. Let me tell you, I'm a horrible artist, but this complex picture is inexplicably the only thing that I've ever been able to draw. When I was flying from Punta Arenas to Puerto Williams in Chile, I had thought again about this image, and was gripped by a powerful feeling that I needed to research it and understand it. And there it was, right before me, in this remote mountaintop village.

The symbol, I soon learned, stands for "unification." According to the Torah, unification "is the pattern through which we can realize the infinite goodness and unconditional love which is the one source of our every moment." As I stood in front of this painting, the concept of love, the name Zohar, and the meaning of this symbol all hit me at once. Sports with my friends, holidays with my grandparents, life lessons from Mom and Dad, and good times with Maya and Ravi were all part of a much larger picture. You could say I had a religious experience, I guess, because I walked away with a far deeper sense of my place in the universe and perhaps even a clue or two about the origin of my soul.

I expected to continue the spiritual enlightenment at the Western Wall, or Wailing Wall, in the Old City of Jerusalem. Many Jews spend their entire lives attempting to get to this holiest of sites, the sole remnant of the ancient temple at the heart of early Jewish worship. The night before, Reut had held us all spellbound with her tale of an army training exercise that had culminated at the Wall. She and other soldiers had been taken on a lengthy nighttime run. At points along the way, they'd stopped to hear their superior officers tell them about various Jews who'd given their lives or made monumental sacrifices so that the State of Israel could be formed. By the time Reut arrived at the Wall, she was at a fever pitch—she told us she just freaked out in anger, full of rage at Israel's enemies, but wanting peace so badly. She broke down in tears, pounded the wall with her fists, and collapsed. It was heartwrenching to watch this tough Israeli soldier weep uncontrollably as she told us this.

The next day, as we walked toward the Wall, I cannot lie—I too was overcome with emotion, overwhelmed by what this wall stands for and how much it means to Israel and to Jews worldwide. I quickly put on my yarmulke, or kipah, as it's called in Israel, and walked right up to it.

As is the custom, I wrote a short note on a piece of paper, stuffed it into a crack in the wall, and raised my right hand—at which point I expected something monumental to occur. I wasn't sure what, but I figured I would start to cry, God might talk to me, or some divine thought would enter my mind. But as I placed my hand on the wall, and then my forehead on it, nothing happened. I tried it again. And again. Nothing.

"Is this thing on?" I asked myself, still expecting something insanely cool to happen. I looked around and suddenly felt awkward, surrounded by praying and bobbing Hasidic Jews wearing tefillin, those small leather boxes they attach to their heads and arms. I still couldn't feel anything. Or so I thought. And I needed to get out of there. I didn't feel ready to take on whatever the wall means to Jews—I felt a lack of real-life experience, at least compared to Reut.

On our final tour day, we went to Yad Vashem, the Holocaust Memorial in Jerusalem, and Mount Herzl, the famous cemetery that sits alongside Yad Vashem. Always a site for solemn introspection, it was today a place of hope and fear. The prisoner exchange between the Israelis and the Palestinians, the Lebanese and Hezbollah was about to come to a head. No one knew if the two Israeli soldiers were still alive—and no one knew how the Palestinians would react to the outcome.

As our group of thirty sat in a small classroom watching a dvd about the Holocaust, Reut received word of the exchange. At the end of the film, she walked to the front of the room and told us that the exchange had occurred. Sadly, the two Israeli soldiers had returned home "in a box," in wooden coffins.

As the news spread, I could only compare it to what it must have been like in the U.S. after the Kennedy assassination. Not in overall scale, but in depth of emotion, when half our nation was angry and half crushed. Some Israelis were furious because they felt the government never should have agreed to an exchange, for their soldiers were likely dead, and Israel was giving Lebanon a convicted murderer in return. Others were in mourning, because they had kept a glimmer of hope that their two Israeli sons would return alive. Emotions were high and Israel was on edge, while the Palestinians celebrated the return of one of their heroes.

I walked around the Holocaust Memorial that day certain that I had to find out more about the Israeli/Palestinian relationship. And the group tour wasn't helping—due to well-founded security concerns, we were kept out of the other three quarters of the Old City, to say nothing of the West Bank. So I went back to my hotel that night to develop a plan with Reut. After that, I went out for a little Jerusalem night life, which may have involved one too many beers, and may have ended with me attempting to hit on a tall, gorgeous Israeli soldier I'd met.

I went to sleep at 5:30 a.m., woke up at 6:15, and set out on my own to the Muslim, Christian, and Armenian Quarters to find out who hated me, and if hate was prevalent. And it sure was.

Granted, it was a time of extreme tension in Jerusalem, but even the Christians gave me attitude. The Armenians stared me down, and the Muslims yelled and cursed. I interpreted this as nothing more than bravado—I certainly wasn't out there looking for a fight. I just wanted answers. Do all other religious groups in Israel really hate the Jews? Is that hatred inevitable and innate? Or is peace the language of the world? The only way to find out was to push the envelope and ask.

And this is a region of no easy answers, not the least of which is what name to give the land on which we stood. Though Palestinians recognize Jerusalem, they do not recognize the State of Israel. Further, the Palestinians are now a people without a country, much as the Jews were before the establishment of Israel after World War II. And for much of the world, Palestine exists in name only. Needless to say, feelings run deep.

Before I had a chance to make progress on my quest, I heard the news emanating from Israel's neighbors. It was not good. Lebanon had given a red-carpet welcome—literally—to the Palestine Liberation Front fighter who had been swapped for the two Israeli bodies. He was also being celebrated throughout the West Bank and Gaza, and appeared on tv to boast he'd do it again. What he and a few others had done, some twenty years earlier, was enter the country by sea, shoot a police officer, and then take hostages, a 28-year-old man and his 4-year-old daughter. He shot the father at close range and, horribly, crushed the girl's head. To compound the tragedy, the mother accidentally suffocated their infant girl while they hid. So yeah,

I was angry and sick to my stomach at seeing this man applauded for his brutality.

"Don't go anywhere—it's hostile out there" was what I heard all around me. But I needed to follow through and find out the truth behind the conventional wisdom that hate is everywhere. So I stopped at an internet café to write e-mails to Coach Carroll and one of my friends from Dalton, Ryan Tierney. I wrote to Coach and to Ryan for the same reason: they would understand.

This, in part, is what I wrote to Ryan:

> *Date: July 16, 2008*
>
> *Hey Ryan...hope all is well back home with your girl and life... it is amazing over here...I've seen so much and been changed a great deal...*
>
> *I need you to be mellow after reading this and be poised...cannot write this to the 3 boys or Ravi...you are the only one who can handle this...things have gotten a little heavy over here with the Hezbollah and Israel and the recent soldier exchange...and you know me, I've got to go check it out...so I'm going in, bro...Trust me, it's NOT stupid... dangerous yes, but stupid, no...you must trust that I know the fine line that exists there and am well prepared...but also trust that in my search for the language of the world, there is no purer way than this... also, trust me that I'll be cool...*
>
> *I've got to find out, man...love ya...kick ass at work...and I'll call you when I return to the states or e-mail you when I have the time to do so...if you do not hear from me by Tuesday then become a surfer and write a book...love ya, brotha...rip it!*
>
> *To thine own self be true.*
>
> *Yogi*

I hit "send" and jumped into a beat-up blue bus, #36, and rode to a stopping point where I found a taxi-van to take me the rest of the way into the West Bank and Jericho. I was pretty much alone in thinking this was a good idea—the other passengers felt free to express their feelings about me quite loudly, in fact. It was intense, and I could do nothing but sit quietly.

We eventually arrived in Jericho and the first thing I wanted to do was turn around and go back to the relative safety of Jerusalem. If there were a time when a Jewish kid could get killed in a place where hatred is supposedly widespread, it would be here and now. But if I took off, I wouldn't be able to prove my "language of the world is peace" theory and dispel a stereotype. So the stakes were high.

Only one man had actually addressed me personally on the ride, so I asked him if I could take him out for lunch. He just walked away. Of course I followed and asked him again. This time he responded with a question.

"What are you doing here, Michael?" he asked, using my name for the day. I had introduced myself as Michael, a writer, because it seemed more normal than Yogi, and well, safer than the truth.

"I want to see Jericho; it's the oldest city in the world."

He asked again, "What are you doing here?"

I took as this an opportunity to lay out my entire theory of peace and how the world does not innately hate. I was Coach Carroll giving a Friday night pre-game speech, and I finished with a flurry of emotion.

Unlike the Trojans, this man stood there motionless, listening. Finally he said, "Michael, you are fucking crazy. Get away from me. You will get both of us killed."

This time I took the hint and headed off to find the nearest taxi back to Jerusalem, but not before grabbing a bite to eat. After all, I was hungry and *Lonely Planet* did say the falafel was great in Jericho.

A bit later I was sitting on a park bench in the center of Jericho, ready for my vegetable wrap, when three men surrounded me. Two flanked me on the bench, but faced the other way, and another stood nearby. I didn't just think that my life was at risk—I thought my head was about to get blown off. In those long moments I thought only of four people: Mom, Dad, Maya, and Ravi. It was a true test of who I was. I couldn't act like a tough guy or show that I was scared. I just had to be myself. So I sat there and waited—for what seemed like an eternity. Eventually the three men moved on, without so much as a nod.

After a few more minutes on the park bench, I decided to find some fruit for the road, so I went to a local stand, run by a young boy and his father. When I paid, I gave the boy some Israeli coins and told him to keep the change. Then this little 8-year-old impressed the daylights out of me. "No, I cannot take!" he boldly stated. This kid, in the middle of a run-down town, had too much pride to take anything he had not earned.

After his father and I chatted for only a few minutes, the man accepted me into the West Bank, as did their friends. I hung all day chatting with locals, laughing with kids, taking pictures with them all, and even spilling the beans about my real name. My theory was proved—deep down we all are predisposed to living in peace—and I was on cloud nine. As the day wound down, I couldn't have been happier, but I also knew I had to bail: it would soon be dark.

From cab to cab I went, but no one wanted to give me a ride. As the sun sank, my anxiety rose. The unwritten rule in the West Bank is that if you are there past sunset, you are in for a wild, even dangerous night under the Middle Eastern stars.

Eventually I found a cab that would take me back to bus #36. As we crossed the military checkpoint, three young Israeli soldiers asked for our identifications. An interesting scenario, as I had been lying to everyone, saying I was Michael, a writer from Los Angeles, not Yogi Zohar Roth, a Jew from Dalton, Pennsylvania.

We all had to pass our ID papers up to the front of the cab. Although the other passengers opened theirs up to the page that indicated name and nationality, I passed mine up closed, and held my breath, hoping none of the Palestinians on board would crack it open. Finally my passport reached a skinny, seemingly 18-year-old soldier who looked like a walk-on defensive back at Pitt. He scrutinized my passport and then stared at me as if to say, "What the hell are you doing here?" I attempted to use the non-verbal communication skills that I'd learned at Pitt, willing him just to hand my papers back to the driver and let us go. Finally, he did.

Full of newfound confidence and swagger, I rode back to Israel, sitting with six Palestinians, and I never felt more comfortable. That is, until we arrived at my bus stop. I was too late—I watched the back of bus #36 as it drove away, leaving dust in my face and the hot sun setting on my now leathery neck.

So I did what any young traveler would do in a similar situation—I hitched a ride. Problem was—I had to pay and the drivers knew it. The guy I settled on seemed like a nice enough fellow, mid-30s, who told me he had a wife and two daughters. We continued to chat amiably until I noticed that we were heading away from the main roads and into the hills. Thinking back to my research on the West Bank, I knew that if my driver veered from the main roads there were two possibilities: 1) there was danger on the highways, or 2) he was going to kill me.

Remember, my goal on this voyage was not to see Jericho or the West Bank, but rather to understand the differences between the Israelis and the Palestinians. So I began to ask questions—questions about the prisoner exchange, the Palestinian government, Israel/Palestine relations, and Islam. He drove faster, trying to ignore me, and snapped a few curt responses. Instead of backing off, I dug deeper. The questions I asked got more specific, more intrusive, and more educated. And his responses got angrier and more resentful.

Well, I thought, if this man is going to kill me, the least I want from him is some knowledge to take with me to the grave. Maybe, also, I pushed him as far as I could because I trusted that he would not in fact kill me. The language of the world is peace. The language of the world is peace. The language of the world is…

"Get out." He suddenly hit the brakes as we neared Jerusalem, and snapped at me.

"Get out? But I'm not in the Old City, I'm not in Israel."

"Forty shekels. This is as far as I go."

So I paid him, stepped out of his van, and looked around. As I turned 360 degrees, I noticed tall white apartment buildings with onlookers leaning against their balconies, drinks in hand, eyes squarely on the kid from Dalton in REI khaki travel pants and a now sweat-stained white button-down shirt. Two birds soared in the air above the desert landscape. Finally, I noticed a large wall that stretched for miles—and could see Jerusalem in the distance. It was then that I realized I was staring at the security fence that separated the West Bank from Israel. It was also then that I whispered to myself, "Fuck me."

This is not the type of wall that one just hops over; it is a wall that marks the separation of not only two religions and cultures, but two global visions. So I started to walk along it, looking for some type of entrance, when a Palestinian soldier yelled at me through a megaphone. What he was saying I wasn't sure, and I really didn't care, as my only focus was on getting into

Israel. When he approached me, I pulled out my passport, and he let me go after a long stare-down.

By now it was almost dark, and I picked up my pace. Soon another driver offered me a ride, and I accepted. After all, he was driving a 5-speed Corolla, just like I did back in Hermosa Beach. So I didn't hesitate to tell him I was headed for the Jewish Quarter. Once again I began to pose my undiplomatic questions, and, once again I got an earful of Palestinian rage, punctuated by clouds of cigarette smoke. As we argued about the Middle East, my goal was to get him to say "Israel," and his was to avoid that at all costs. Like his predecessor, he soon hit the brakes and told me to get out—and to pay him what was apparently the going rate of forty shekels, of course.

Surprisingly, I had finally reached the Old City, though I was nowhere near the Jewish Quarter. My goal was to go back to the Wailing Wall, where my day had begun, because I knew the Wall would be a place of worship and peace, because the funerals for the two soldiers had been held earlier that day.

So I headed into the nearest quarter, the Muslim Quarter, and met people and struck up conversations, going through the final test of my theory. You see, if they were as angry or hostile as everyone had told me, then there would be no chance for me, a young Jewish-American man, to even make it through alive.

But I passed in relative peace—I drew just a few dirty looks and negative comments as I made my way back to the Wall via first the Muslim Quarter, and then the Armenian and Christian quarters. When I finally reached the Wall and placed my head against it, I felt Israel. And I felt Jewish.

But somehow I kept the West Bank and the Palestinians with me as well. I had no red string bracelet, because I had ripped it off in Jericho to hide my identity. I wore no kipah, as it didn't feel right. Just my hand and forehead on the wall. And what I felt was simply pride. Pride in my heritage. Pride in my name. Pride in my grandparents. Pride in my mom, as I stood with honor for her homeland, and mine.

Looking back in my journal to see what I wrote then, I find this:

> *July 17, 2008, was the greatest day in my life as it was a day where I saw two nations that love to love life. But I also saw two nations who must know how to **hate** to survive in life.*

So my day fulfilled that urge to live on the edge of danger while trying to learn. But what now? Did I find an answer to this world issue? I don't know. As I sit and write here on the stone floor of the Old City staring at the Wailing Wall with tears in my eyes, I just don't know.

The hardest part is not only realizing that peace between these two worlds is nearly impossible, but it is also looking at the children who play in the streets of Israel and Palestine. We don't look at them and see cute kids, for, as Reut said, "We don't have babies...We have soldiers."

That thought is crazy and it kills me. But I do know that there must be a plan before there is a solution, and it starts with one person believing and then communicating. So I guess the answer to "what now?" would be to gain a voice, try to change the world, and try to find the language of the world, the soul of the world, by listening to my own heart.

Let the world change you...and you can change the world.

As the sun finally set, I walked out of the Old City toward the business district, and was drained mentally, emotionally, and physically. But I also was at peace, as my travels proved that whether I was in Dalton, L.A., or Israel, society at heart wants to live in harmony. A simple thought, and one that makes perfect sense.

And then I hopped onto a bus for Tel Aviv. There, with the bright lights and non-stop urban energy, I felt both rejuvenated and exhausted as I hit a dance club with some new friends.

And the next day I surfed. The best waves I'd seen since Bali. Epic.

PART III
USC

REM SLEEP

22

Each season is a lifetime.
We are either immortal and win every game,
or dead and reborn the following August.
This is my final lifetime.

I WALK INTO COACH CARROLL'S OFFICE on a cool December morning in 2008, and I can sense something about to happen. A burrito is passed to me from our player personnel director Jared Blank, like Montana to Rice, and I take my seat on Coach's new brown leather chair. He sits on the couch, unwraps his burrito and takes a bite too big for his mouth. He chews, then sets his burrito down on the coffee table, which is covered with action shots of his players.

"Yogi, what's up, man?" he says with a chuckle.

"Not much, Coach, you?"

"Well, I want to ask you a question…."

I nod.

"Do you want to be the next full-time quarterbacks coach at USC?"

And then I wake up. Every time I wake up at that exact moment. Can Freud, Maslow, or even *Men's Health* please explain that? Can they please explain this dream? Signal callers are the CEOs, yet the hardest workers; the leaders in the locker room, but normal guys in their meeting room; an extension of the staff on the field, but the furthest thing from a coach in the huddle. They are the quarterbacks; they have a unique presence. They are a special breed.

Well, even if I'm not the new full-time QB coach at USC as my subconscious would like, I do know that this fall will be the greatest yet. It is August, our team is primed, our quarterbacks are ready, and I have never ever been more excited for a season to begin. Either I know my gig's about to come to an end, or I'm falling in love with coaching ball. And whatever the case, I've decided to document this season—record the ins and outs of coaching with Carroll, 2008-09.

TRAINING CAMP

23

DATE: August 4, 2008
SUBJECT: Letters

Dear Ravi,

So my fourth season at USC has begun. With training camp underway, I can honestly say that heading into this season I've never been more excited. As you know, I like to write, and I journal throughout each season, but it's typically inconsistent at best. So I thought: what better way to move through this season than by writing letters to you a few times per week. The plan is once training camp ends, I'll shoot you an e-mail Friday night before the game, Sunday morning after the game, and Monday night as we are preparing for the upcoming opponent.

Why you? Well, that's simple. You live in New York City, you're an actor, you face tough odds every day, you compete every moment you breathe as auditions and competition define your daily life. And like our 2008-09 squad, you relish the moment to perform, and you dream of competing at the highest level (Broadway). At the same time, you would act in our backyard for free, just as our players would play ball in front of 50 fans with the same juice as in front of 92,000.

You see, you act for the purity of performance. We coach and play for the purity of the game. Now, I can't lie and say that the fanfare, 92,000 fans, ESPN highlights, and fun nights in Hermosa Beach are not awesome, just as you cannot look me in the eye and say that the autographs you sign, the potential of being in US! *Magazine*, or maybe winning a Tony don't get you a little jacked.

Thus, little bro, we essentially live in the same world, sip from the same competitive juice box, and love to put on a show. The only difference is that you are singing and dancing and I am talking ball on a headset.

So, welcome to my book. I hope you don't mind, as I've not asked your permission to make you be a part of it, but if you don't agree, I'll just beat on you like I used to—lol.

Talk soon and keep dreaming,

Yogi

P.S. Will anyone else enjoy this? I have no clue. All I know is that training camp is on the horizon, and you are about to join me on a five-month journey that will feel like a lifetime.

P.P.S. I'll try to keep the letters short.

DATE: August 5, 2008
SUBJECT: Training Camp 2008

Dear Ravi,

Today our players reported for training camp. Easily the longest day in the history of ball. I cleaned my desk more times than I did as a child, and my locker is more organized than Dad's filing cabinets.

We met as a staff this morning and spoke about our team's major challenge this year, which is far tougher than just our schedule. It's the teaching. How do we get our players to perform with greatness? How do we teach them well?

The answer? First, we must not fight the fact that, like you, we are entertainers. We need to keep their attention by inspiring them through more than coach rhetoric. Through video, internet, jokes, and other voices, we must teach. The last six Pac-10 titles proved that athletes will go as far as their leaders take them, and, believe it or not, I am one of those leaders. And I am one of the few on our staff who know how to edit entertaining videos. But whatever.

Some things we have to keep in mind are:

1) start all the players off on a clean slate,
2) let the competition sort itself out, and,
3) most important, have a blast throughout it all.

I'll tell ya, man, something I have learned here is that a good teacher makes a better learner. And in sports, as well as in acting, the roles of teacher and learner can often flip-flop.

The evening meeting began with the players singing Dennis Slutak's version of Snoop Dogg's "Drop It Like It's Hot". Dennis is director of football operations here, and not technically a rapper, so it was pretty hilarious. This was followed by an administrative meeting where the players were told how important bed check is, how they must respect everything, how to nourish their bodies over the next 28 practices, and how agents are the devils and their runners are the SARS virus. Oh, and how could I forget—we taught them about the ladies. In sum, "If you're going rabbit hunting and the rabbit is chasing you, stay away from that rabbit."

After dinner the real meeting finally began. This is where Coach Carroll set the tone for training camp and the season. Of course, he did it in classic PC fashion, with great style, energy and an ability to have our team loose yet extremely focused, as if the pressure that others talked of regarding our season never even existed.

I'm off to bed.

Yogi

DATE: August 6, 2008
SUBJECT: Respect

Ravi,

What is respect? A good question, huh? We asked our players about it last night and the answer was unanimous: "It's what everyone wants."

I couldn't agree more, but let's take it one step further. When you respect something, you value it. You can't choose when or when not to respect something/someone. Thus, respect everything.

Rip it,

Yogi

DATE: August 8, 2008
SUBJECT: QB

Dear Ravi,

Today the hearts of the Trojan faithful skipped a beat. Their golden arm, the player whom I've gotten to know over the past three years, was carried off the field and driven to the local hospital. Our starting quarterback, the man who would follow the path laid out ever so brilliantly by Carson Palmer, Matt Leinart, and John David Booty, was done. It was as though a lunar eclipse came over Los Angeles, and it was in the form of Mark Sanchez's collapsed left knee.

I can't lie. When I saw him being carried off, I thought, "He must have cramped up." Ten minutes later Coach Carroll walked over to me and told me that Mark's kneecap was dislocated and it would be 4-6 weeks. My mind immediately went to our schedule, and I knew that 4-6 weeks meant 2-4 games. In the sport of college football, that is a lifetime.

But after that moment of "oh no" passed, the *Win Forever* philosophy of Pete Carroll resurfaced, and I knew we would be fine, as our back-ups are more than capable, and this is a beautiful opportunity for them to compete.

It's really similar to you when you were in the off-Broadway show *Altar Boyz*. After the lead went down with a vocal chord issue, you were called upon to replace him in what was easily your largest role. What did you do? You competed, prepared, and kicked ass. I know our back-ups, now potential starters, will do the same.

I'm off to bed, bro,

Yogi

P.S. Coach just told us that the diagnosis is a dislocated kneecap, and Mark will be back in ten days. So you can now see how I can rest easy....

DATE: August 9, 2008
SUBJECT: Coffee (joe)

Ravi,

Goal is to have less than ten cups of joe this season. Today was numero uno.

Yogi

DATE: August 10, 2008
SUBJECT: Dorms

Ravi,

So I got busted. Royally busted.

Last night I just needed to go home. About a week into camp and I just wanted to cruise home for the night. Let me tell you my normal schedule. Wake up at 6:30 AM, walk to the office, take a shower while I'm trying to squeeze in a few more minutes of REM sleep while standing up, throw on my coaching gear for the day, put contacts in, turn on both of my computers, grab breakfast (fyi – French toast sticks are awesome this camp!), and head to the staff meeting. After a day of coaching, meeting, and watching film, I usually stroll back to the dorm around midnight. There, Jared Blank, Justin Mesa, Al Dorsey, Randall Green, and I talk about the day, and around 1:15 AM I jump into bed. Literally, I jump, as it's a dorm bed that is raised about 4 feet. Stupid, yes, but it's one more competitive moment each day. I then set three alarms (cell, clock, and watch). Afterwards I usually lay there for a few minutes, text a few friends, and ultimately pass out. I repeat the process the next day.

The point is that I'm supposed to stay in the dorms as the "coaching presence." Well, bed check is 11:00 PM, and most players are passed out by 11:30 PM, so when I finally arrive at the dorm, no one is even awake. So last night, I thought I would just cruise home, get a good night's sleep, and feel great today. I couldn't have been more off the mark.

So backtrack for a moment to last night, when a staff member asked me if I was going home. I replied, "I should stay."

His response: "Why? No one knows if you're there anyway. Just go home tonight. You need a good night's sleep."

So I obliged. But as I walked into the office this morning, I got a call from Coach Carroll.

"Yogi, what happened last night?"
"Mmm…I don't know, Coach."
"At the dorms. LAPD showed up looking for Kyle Moore and he ran. No one can find him. You were there, right?"
"Mmm…I don't know, Coach."

Yeah, yeah—great response right?

So I hung up and went to find answers. I called Jared, Justin, Al, and Randall. No love from any of them. I was now in full guilty mode. You know me: I take pride in not being the one who screws up, and now the night I decided to be selfish and sneak home, a player got arrested.

So I called Coach back. "Coach, no one knows where Kyle is."

"OK Yogi, I gotta go. LAPD is on the other line." His stern, no-nonsense tone made me feel about the size of my little bedbug friends in the dorms.

When Coach eventually showed up at work, I knew that I needed to come clean. So I walked into his office and tried to tell him, but Slu walked in, and Coach kicked me out, as they needed to meet.

More time passed, and the guilt got worse. OK, I know, what's the big deal? But Coach and I have a cool relationship, and I just had to tell him.

After a half hour, he called me into his office. There, he explained that Kyle is in a piracy ring and has been tracked for months. Halfway through his explanation, I stopped him. "Coach, I got to tell you. I went home last night. It won't happen again."

He looked at me like Dad would when I disappointed him, and I walked out.

Next was a team meeting, where he told the squad about Kyle and the trouble he's in. About five minutes into his explanation, he broke out that it was just a joke and that we were cancelling practice to go bowling. Well, not only was the team jacked about his prank, but also the staff was on their backs laughing, as his joke got me.

So, thanks to that unnamed staff member, some mentor and friend, huh!

And yes, I'll be sleeping in the dorms tonight, with my little friends.

Yogi

DATE: August 11, 2008
SUBJECT: Bo Taylor

August 11, 2008 - The day the world became a better place.
August 11, 2008 - The day the world said good-bye to a legend.
August 11, 2008 - The day Bo Taylor's legacy became immortal.

Dear Ravi,

I was working on a fake field goal with the kickers today when Jared ran up to me. He was winded and flushed. Jared is the type of guy who would never interrupt anyone because he is A) too nice and B) way too nice.

"Yogi, can I talk to you for a second?"

"Sure, man, what is it?" I asked as we walked away from the specialists.

"Bo passed today...."

I'm not sure what he said after that, but I'll always remember those first three words.

"Bo" is Bo Taylor. He is the gang interventionist in Los Angeles. Bo Taylor is to the streets what Pete Carroll is to football.

He is a rockstar, a legend, a prodigy. He saves kids' lives by teaching them that there are more than two ways (jail and death) out of the streets.

For 17 years Bo has been a legend on the streets of LA. From the Watts Towers to the Jungle, Bo is respected. And over the past few years, he and Coach have become the best of friends, busting each other like brothers, laughing at inside jokes, giving each other the cheap nudges you know all too well. They've also supported each other. When we've lost, I'm sure Bo is one of the first calls on Coach's cell phone, and as Bo battled cancer for the past few months, Coach was the one challenging him to compete each day.

I've been able to talk and hang with Bo these last three months. At first Bo was just a legend who came into the office every week. Everyone wanted to be his boy—you know, one of the guys whom Bo would say, 'What up?' to. As time went on, his visits became news. "Did you hear Bo was in the office today?" "Did you see Bo today?"

He had that "It" factor. Like a quarterback from Pennsylvania or a point guard from the Bronx or the lead in *Phantom*, Bo had "It."

So I ran from the practice field into Coach's office. He was on the phone, with everyone around him crying, burying their heads in their hands, or unsure of how to react to the news of Bo's passing.

I didn't have much time to talk to Coach since practice was about to begin, but I could see the pain in his eyes.

Practice #7 came and went as we worked on short yardage and goal line situations. After practice, it was position meetings, and finally, here I sit at my desk at 11:42 PM.

My heart is aching, but I can't stop smiling. I know, I know, you're saying, "Yogi, you don't have to be so tough." But I'm not trying to be. I'm sure tears will come at some point, but now I can't stop smiling.

Why? Well, because of the two moments that keep flashing before my eyes.

First, about a month ago, Bo and I had met with a television producer about a reality program that he would host, and afterwards we had talked about this peace march and rally that Coach Carroll spearheads. For two hours, he and his daughter had sat with me in my office while he had told me about the streets of Los Angeles. He had spoken about what is going on, how he and Coach are changing communities, and how Unity I (his program) and A Better LA (Coach's organization) are on the verge of truly changing a culture in Los Angeles.

As one of the organizers for the march and rally (Along with Amber Carroll, Jaime Carroll, Angela Carter, and many others), I had given Bo the pitch on the event, titled LA LIVEPEACE 08. I had laid out the plan and the logistics that our team had come up with, and he had told me who should and, more important, who should not speak.

I need to pause for a minute and paint you a picture of Bo. Basically, think of the coolest guy on the planet. Seriously, I don't even know how to describe his coolness factor. His voice, for instance, was just awesome! It was that mix between the guy who gets all of the beautiful women by just saying "Hi" and the man whose skin exudes inspiration. Add to that, he is the only person I know who can pull off wearing shades *indoors*. If Bo Taylor had a Q-rating, his score would be through the roof.

Like a Heisman Trophy-winning quarterback, Bo had a presence.

Anyway, back to the story. So there we were, the three of us, at USC in the staff room, and Bo had signed off on the event. For the next 30 minutes, I was absolutely blown away as he made phone call after phone call.

"Alex, I need ya, man. It's about to happen."
"Blinky, it's time. We've got to call the crew."
"Aquil, we've talked about this for a long time and it's really happening."
"Chief Beck, it's time to make a statement."

Each response was the same, as if on cue. And, thankfully, on speakerphone.

"Bo, I'm in. Anything for you. We'll be there. I love ya, man."

After Bo walked out of the office that afternoon with his daughter, I walked back to my desk, sat down and just stared at a blank computer screen. It was then that I knew that this peace rally was for real, that Bo Taylor was for real, and that we better not screw this event up!

August 2, 2008, finally arrived, and LA LIVEPEACE 08 was in full force as this day would serve as my second memorable moment with Bo. The Coke truck, Quiksilver t-shirts, Power 106 live music, a stage, and much more were ready by 7:00 AM. The march was set to begin at 10:00, and the rally to follow at 11:00.

I had the honor of driving Bo on the march in a USC golf cart. When I picked him up at his car, this man couldn't stop crying. He was overcome with emotion and joy. This was the day that he had dreamed of.

Sure, Bo had been to, spoken at, and organized many peace marches and rallies, but this one had a different feel for him. Could it have been the sponsorship? Maybe. The publicity? Possibly. Because *60 Minutes* was there? Perhaps. Because the mayor of San Francisco announced his run for governor there? Highly doubtful.

If I were a betting man, my money would be on the fact that when Bo entered the event peristyle end of the Los Angeles Memorial Coliseum for the opening press conference at 9:45 AM, he knew that this event would change others, that this statement of peace in the streets of LA would prove to him that the majority of his life was a HUGE success, and that this would be his final lap on Martin Luther King Boulevard.

As we rode down Figueroa Street, took a right on MLK, and another on Hoover before entering the Coliseum, Bo turned to me.

"Yogi, I can honestly say that I can die a happy man."

"Bo, you're not going anywhere," I replied.

"I know, I know, I'm going to fight this thing, but I can really say I'm not afraid of death. Look at this, man! Look at the streets! The smile it puts on my face and in my heart is amazing. It is happening, man. The culture is changing!"

Bo continued, "And Yogi, I want to say that I love you. You are a chosen one, like Pete. You guys have to keep this going. You're with me, man—no matter what."

The rest of the march was a relative blur, as well-wishers, friends, and photographers surrounded Bo and gave him the celebrity treatment only a peacekeeper deserves.

As we made our final turn on Hoover, Byron Pitts of *60 Minutes* asked Bo a question.

"Bo, what do you want in life?"

Bo's answer was classic Bo. It wasn't "I want to beat throat cancer" or "I want to live to be 100" or "I want to be a millionaire."

It was Bo Taylor as only Bo Taylor could be.

In his cool voice and brown Maui Jim's, Bo said ever so softly, "I want peace, man...peace."

And with that simple thought, we need to realize that life is that easy. Life is that simple.

We make it complex. With our analyzing and our over-thinking, our statistics and our policy changes, we have turned this world into a maze with no end. Yet we can bring it back, and Bo's life can serve as a blueprint.

Bo Taylor easily made the decisions that others think are hard because he trusted the most God-given thing in this world—his heart. He listened to it, he loved with it, and he changed the streets of Los Angeles and beyond because of it.

On August 11, 2008, Bo Taylor is living peace.
On August 11, 2008, Bo Taylor became more influential than ever before.
On August 11, 2008, Bo Taylor became immortal.

And on August 12, 2008, at 12:27 AM, Bo Taylor finally got me to shed a tear.

Classic Bo Taylor.

DATE: August 15, 2008
SUBJECT: Greatness

Ravi,

Congrats on your extension! Are you the most popular character in *Altar Boyz* yet? Heard you are doing great as one of the leads. But no matter what your fans say, remember who has the best voice in the family.

We are in the middle of training camp and I can honestly say that the dorms are getting old. Quick summation, our starting QB got hurt, our back-ups are playing like...well, back-ups. Our OL is average, as we are having trouble with gap protection (the most basic of all), our RBs are awesome, TEs are killing it, and the defense is, well, ridiculous. All in all, it's a typical training camp with highs and lows.

Tonight, in our team meeting, we spoke of what it means to be great. Something that obviously relates to your profession because, in the end, players in both of our worlds live to perform at an elite level. We love the bright lights, the roar of the crowd, the anticipation of the show, and the challenge of doing it time after time. A few people on our staff spoke tonight. One in particular, Johnny Morton, or Johnny Mo, used to coach Jerry Rice. As you well know, Rice has been my idol for years because his work ethic separated him from the rest. But more than that, and what you can pull from our team meeting, is that great players don't care just about championships; they care about performing each and every time out. It's as though they yearn to prove to others that they are worthy of being dubbed 'great.'

Each time you sing a line or perform a scene, or every time our QBs throw a pass or call a play, you get an opportunity to show who you are, and that is what performance is all about—showing ten, twenty, five hundred, ninety-two thousand, or ten million people who you are and what your make-up is all about. And if you are a competitor who strives to be great, then you will hold onto those moments with everything in your power.

As you may or may not have read in my master's degree thesis, I wrote that to be great one must remain Independent and Consistent. Independent in thought, as that is what gives you a unique edge, and Consistent in approach, as that is necessary for success. Now you will obviously evolve over time in your mindset and approach, but it must remain authentic.

So I guess what I'm telling you at 12:47 AM on the fifteenth of August is that A) I would rather write you a long e-mail than lie in my dorm room bed, and B) every time you step on stage remember that you are given the opportunity to prove who you are and that you've earned that chance. It's a powerful thing to show what you represent, and you must hold onto that with a great deal of seriousness.

Keep rippin', man, and congrats on the extension of your contract in your show.

Yogi

DATE: August 16, 2008
SUBJECT: Women and Training Camp

Almost done with camp. But let me remind you that camp is not much different for a coach than for a player when it comes to the female species.

I don't care who you are: 18-hour days with the same 105 guys can get monotonous and the same gals get better looking by the day. By the tenth day of camp, the trainers look like *Sports Illustrated* models, each lunch lady transforms into the girl next door, and the reporters become runway models.

So yeah, I'm looking forward to going home in another day to see some new faces.

Sorry, bro, but I'm human.

Yogi

DATE: August 18, 2008
SUBJECT: Bedbugs

Ravi,

I woke up at 4:30 in the morning itching like crazy on my back. I swear something was crawling on me. I fell back into a sweaty sleep and woke at 6:30 to check out and cruise home for a few hours to shower and sneak in a quick surf. Dorm life is over!

Yogi

DATE: August 18, 2008
SUBJECT: Joe #2

Ravi,

Had cup #2 today.

Yogi

DATE: August 20, 2008
SUBJECT: Mock Game

Ravi,

Tomorrow is our final scrimmage of Fall Camp 2008. We are staying in the Marriott near LAX as we mimic a road game. It's actually a blast as we practice what it's like the night before a game. From meetings to dinner to chapel service—our players get to practice everything before opening night. Much like a final dress rehearsal.

This is my favorite night in football. Well, nothing can compare to games, but this night is powerful, as I feel it is the pinnacle before the games. I love it so much because after this final meeting every player goes to his hotel room, brushes his teeth, goes to the bathroom, etc., but they all share one moment. It's when you are alone in the bathroom and you look in the mirror. Here you are, face to face with yourself, and there is no room for excuses. You get to look yourself in the eye and tell yourself that you did everything possible to prepare, or you must look yourself in the eye and accept that you could have done more. Essentially, it is the moment where you say "I'm ready" or "I'm screwed."

In my playing career, this night served as a huge moment because preparation was the most important thing for me. Only once, against Syracuse, did I look into the mirror and know that I hadn't prepared as much as I could've. It was the worst feeling in my career, and I stayed up until 4:00 AM studying my playbook just so I could walk onto the field without a single regret. I would have been fine, as I likely knew more than any other receiver, but I needed the feeling of being free and knowing that I had earned the right to walk on that field the next day.

What also makes this night magnificent is the speech that Coach Carroll gives. This is the final time the entire team is truly together before the game, listening to one message.

Tonight, he spoke about how he has given over 500 'night before the game' speeches and the ones at USC have been so special. Oklahoma, Texas, UCLA, Notre Dame, etc. These nights have been a major staple in USC history. His point tonight was that the desire to win and compete never turns off. And because it never turns off, we cannot choose when to perform, when to be "on."

Much like you in acting. You cannot say that "tonight I'm going to give a great solo or have my best performance." Reason being, every night needs to be your final performance, your championship performance. Great performers live for these moments because these moments prove who they are.

To play in a game is the greatest gift we could ask for because we get to prove who we are. It never matters who we play, when we play, or where we play. We just do what we do, and although that may be common, we become uncommon through doing it.

My point is that this uncommon process of playing great each time out does not just happen. You must first have a belief in yourself, and you get that through preparation and practice. From there, you become confident: you trust your approach and plan. After you have gained a belief, confidence, and trust, you can play freely and play with the knowledge that you will succeed.

Once you play free, your love for the game shines through. And love, my little bro, is the clearest thought in this world we live in.

Love what you do, bro, and dare to be great.

I'm off to bed as I'm calling plays tomorrow for the third team offense.

Rip it,

Yogi

P.S. Remember my boy Santiago, hero of *The Alchemist* (the book I made you read)? It's funny, but stories from his journey pop into my head from time to time, ever since traveling in Israel.

DATE: August 23, 2008
SUBJECT: Camp is OVER

Ravi,

Training camp is officially over. Yes, the e-mails about the dorms will end, and our QB is on the mend, so I'm gonna hop into my new Toyota Corolla, cruise to El Porto to surf, and then head home to Hermosa Beach.

Virginia in one week!

Yogi

P.S. Mom and Dad are going to the game.

University of Virginia

24

DATE: August 24, 2008
SUBJECT: Game Plan

Ravi,

Sitting at my desk wondering what you're doing. The season has officially begun as I just finished drawing and correcting 66 pass plays that we are installing for our first game against Virginia. A boring and mundane task when I sit in front of a computer screen and draw lines in various directions, but when those lines are run by real people and real players, the Trojans dominate.

Also, Sark, Coach Carroll, and I met with the back-up quarterback tonight. We had to tell him that he was in fact, going to be a backup. A cool situation since we, as a staff, wanted to be honest with the kid as that is obviously best for the player.

Like Dad said, "Honesty is the best policy." Or was that Mark Twain? Whatever.

I would write more, but I'm beat, hungry, and need some sleep.

Love ya, man,

Yogi

P.S. Oh yeah, so I went out last night, made a full-on attempt to dance, met a cool girl from Brentwood, slept until 11:15, worked out for a few minutes before realizing that my headache was not going away, called the girl from last night to see what was up, went to work, am about to leave work…and yes, you guessed it…still no call back.

At least we can laugh about it.

DATE: August 28, 2008
SUBJECT: Obama

Ravi,

Who inspires you? Who truly inspires you? Is it our parents? Your mentors? Tony-, Oscar- and Emmy-winning actors? Your peers auditioning every day hoping for that break they often dream of? All of the above?

For me it is, of course, our parents and grandparents, but on a political front I've never been inspired during my lifetime. Ever since high school when I was president of the student body, I've liked politics, but never had a person to look up to. At Pitt, I would walk down the large steps in front of the Masonic Temple and give ad-lib speeches, pretending that I was running for president and addressing thousands on that plush green lawn. From there I worked for a state representative and the city's mayor, so I got to see how politics worked at that level, but still, I had no one alive to admire.

I then got interested in 60s politics, as I learned about how many individuals of that era began to change society through their viewpoints—from Bobby Kennedy and Martin Luther King, Jr., to Che Guevara and Nelson Mandela.

Last season, on one of those late nights in the office, Coach Carroll and I sat near my little desk and talked about politics and what it means to change society. I asked him if he wanted to run for office, since he can obviously change a culture. He said "No." Curious, I pushed for an explanation. His response was simple: "To change a culture you do not have to run for office; you just have to get people to believe, to listen, to become inspired." And so his foundation, A Better LA, has taken off. It was on that platform that we had our peace rally over the summer.

Anyway, Coach's response that night stuck with me. He was right. You don't need to have a major title or a big office in Washington, DC, to make change. Rather, you just have to get people to listen. To do that, you keep your message simple and, yes, you guessed it, you gotta speak from the heart.

Also on that night I realized that no living political figure has ever inspired me, ever made me want to emulate him or her, ever made me a believer. (Clinton was the closest.)

And that is when I truly became a Barack Obama fan.

Tonight, as I sit on my hotel bed in Charlottesville, Virginia, with Mom and Dad sound asleep in the bed adjacent to mine, I can say that I am inspired. I can say that, for the first time in my lifetime, a political figure who is alive has captured me.

Obama spoke about change, about leadership, and about how he will lead our nation. He took on all of the pundits' critiques and questions and stared them straight in the eye. He looked over 80 million people in the face and told them how he will lead his nation and the world at a time when it needs leadership the most. And he told them in a simple, old-school fashion—one that was from the heart.

You see, I believe that many people can successfully lead teams, states, and countries as long as their players or constituents like them. But to *inspire*, to *change* a culture, to *dare to be great*, those coaches or leaders must be **loved**. Tonight, while watching Barack Obama's acceptance speech at the Democratic National Convention, I found out that Obama is loved by this country. His counterpart, like many past politicians, is only liked (at best).

Throughout his speech, I kept saying to Mom and Dad, "He just said what?!" as Obama went for it. He made bold statements, stark distinctions, and honest declarations. But at the end, one thing that he said really stuck with me:

"Throughout this entire election people have made this about race, my opinion, etc... but to be honest—this election is not about me, it's about YOU."

Obama got me with that statement. You see, Ravi, he realizes that if one gives in life, deflects praise to others, remains humble, and is not afraid to share his success with others, then the admiration and love he gets in return is ten-fold. And in Obama's case—it is million-fold.

Lastly, you must know that there is no cookie cutter way to success. There is no cookie cutter way to be great. We, the future of this nation, the future of Broadway (you!), must continue to think outside of the box, we must continue to take chances, and we must do it without fear. So when you wake up and read this, if you have an audition or a performance later tonight—do me a favor. Let it rip, and remember that it is your unique style that brought you to the stage you are performing on. Trust your instincts, listen to your heart, and be true to yourself, as that will attract your fans and, in some cases, a nation toward your beliefs and performances.

Tonight, bro, I was inspired. Tonight, I listened to a man who listened to his heart. Tonight, Barack Obama spoke to the world in what my friend Santiago would call the *language of the world*.

Tonight was special.

Love ya, man!

Yogi

P.S. Maybe I'll run for office someday.

_____

DATE: August 29, 2008
SUBJECT: "I'm gonna go off tomorrow"

Ravi,

Opening game is one day away. The boys are jacked and I am fired up. Over the last few years, my yearning to play has lessened, but this game, the opener against Virginia, is one in which I would love to play.

We just got back from our walk-thru at their stadium and it was classic. As we stood on the sideline, our strength and conditioning coach, Chris Carlisle, gave the boys a speech. It is tradition that he talks to the team at every away game and gives them a speech discussing history. It is usually about a battle that occurred, and in only Coach C fashion, it ties beautifully into the vibe of our team at that particular time. I think he should be a professor, as his messages are clear and awesome: they fire us up.

Anyway, as we were listening to his talk, Virginia's team walked out onto the field. You must understand that both teams' being on the field the day before the game is about as good a mix as beer, liquor, and three slices of Pizano's on a Saturday night at 1:00 AM. I thought disaster was about to strike as one of their players was sure to start chirping, and an all-out brawl was imminent.

Thankfully, nothing happened, as neither team said anything. But the psychological game that was played was magnificent.

Let me paint a picture for you. We are standing on _their_ sideline as they walk out for their walk-thru. We remain on _their_ sideline, and they stand on the visitor sideline looking like they've just seen a ghost.

After Coach Carlisle's speech, the boys came together and broke it down one time with our new chant. UVA's players just stood there and did nothing. I am standing there almost pleading with them to speak up! I mean, have some guts! Pretend! Fake it! Act, for God's sake!

But they just turned around and walked back out of their home stadium without even breathing on _their_ home field sideline.

OK, not a big deal, right? Wrong! We, for lack of a better phrase, just punk'd them on *their* home turf!

If I were with UVA, I would have walked my ass right over to *my* sideline and reminded the visiting players that they were in *my* house.

Walking out of the stadium, one of our new players, Damian Williams, came up to me and said, "I'm gonna go off tomorrow."

That got me thinking and, more important, it got me listening to the rest of our offensive players. It seemed to be a common theme: every player wanted to "go off."

In our team meeting that night, Coach Sarkisian and Coach Carroll both touched on that sentiment, making it clear to the players that "going off" did not mean catching 7 passes or scoring 3 touchdowns or making 10 tackles. What "going off" meant was blocking downfield on a long scoring run, making that tough catch in traffic, blocking the blitzing Sam linebacker, or filling your assigned gap on defense.

We had to get across to the players that if everyone does his job, then we all get to "go off." But if we become individually focused, then we become selfish and further from a team.

In his pre-game address, Coach Carroll spoke of the challenge he issued during training camp to become a great team. The challenge of coming together and playing for one another—of playing as a unit, as a tribe.

To do that, he explained that we must control only what is within our grasp. We cannot worry about the Atlantic Coast Conference officials because we can't control them. We cannot worry about the student section because we can't control them. We cannot worry about the score in the first quarter because we cannot control it. We can only worry about our individual assignments, for it is "all about us."

Not sure if you know, but there is a Native American concept called long body. It means that whatever one member of the tribe feels, the others do as well. For instance, if a person is sick, then they all feel his/her pain. If a person is joyous, then they all feel happy, etc. Eventually, due to long body, the members of a tribe become tightly connected.

The same can be said of our 2008-09 team. When CJ Gable went down with a hip injury, the rest of the team felt it. When Mark Sanchez hurt his knee, the rest of the program sensed it. That concept of long body made Native American tribes closer, and it is a concept that will allow a room of 105 young men to become one unit, one team, one heartbeat.

Tomorrow, we go to battle for the first time.

Tomorrow, we make our first impression on the college football landscape.
Tomorrow, we get to show who we are.
Tomorrow, we get to celebrate.

As Coach Carroll said so enthusiastically at the end of our meeting, "Let's make sure people feel the Trojans."

I'm out,

Yogi

DATE: August 30, 2008
SUBJECT: Game

Dear Ravi,

We destroyed Virginia 52-7. Five tailbacks scored touchdowns, four quarterbacks played, we had over 500 yards of offense, and the Trojans made a statement. We are for real, we are fast, and we have weapons on our team.

While Virginia was horrible, we did not make mistakes that could've hurt us, and we looked relatively sharp in our first game. Ohio State is next after a bye, and it is the most talked-about game in college football, as they have appeared in the last two national championship games.

Exciting—yes.
A big deal—no.

Every game we play is huge, and every game we play is championship-like, so to make this one a bigger deal than any other would be crazy.

Just got to go practice one day at a time, for, as Sark would likely say, "We only have to beat Ohio State today because that's all we got."

It was great seeing Mom and Dad, as well as Vince, who drove to the game. Nate and Justin from Australia were there along with Joe Stephens (wideout at Pitt, #81) and his new bride, Kim.

I'm taking a nap as I'm exhausted and we have a five-hour flight ahead of us.

Love ya, man,

Yogi

THE O-H-I-O STATE UNIVERSITY

25

DATE: September 4, 2008
SUBJECT: Republican Convention

Ravi,

I hope you got to watch the Republican National Convention tonight when Senator John McCain spoke. A lesson to you if you ever produce: don't ever have a green screen behind a speaker because it looks tacky and cheap.

While I am an Obama fan, I really tried to give McCain a chance tonight, but I thought his rhetoric was horrible. If you recall, I did study Greek rhetoric in college and am fascinated by the power of communication and speech, and McCain was not impressive. It will be interesting to see what happens in the next few months, but I'll tell you...get involved, man!

This is a huge time for our generation, and there is a chance for us to have a profound effect on our nation and the world. Get your absentee ballot and let's go, bro!

Obama is going to beat McCain like the Trojans are going to beat up on the Buckeyes!

Love ya, bro,

Yogi

P.S. Obama might come to practice before the election! (Should I tell him I plan on sitting in his seat in twenty years?) Haha.

DATE: September 9, 2008
SUBJECT: Joe #3

Ravi,

Had third cup of joe today. It was awhile since the last one, so get off my case.

Yogi

DATE: September 10, 2008
SUBJECT: Game

Ravi,

Big game this week. The Ohio State Buckeyes are coming to town and we couldn't be more jacked. Not sure what will happen on game day, but we have been working hard this week preparing. Game plan is aggressive and full of shots. They blitz a ton and most teams will either audible away from the pressure or call plays that are away from pressure. Not us. Our plan: attack the pressure when it comes as we are almost welcoming it. An interesting concept as we know what they'll do and we can't wait for them to do it…. Few more days of game planning. Mom and Dad just got here, too.

Yogi

DATE: September 12, 2008
SUBJECT: Friday Night

Dear Ravi,

Friday night. Oh, how special these nights are.

Tonight, the message was loud and clear. Who are we? Who are we collectively?

And here is how our players answered that question:

"We know how to finish."
"We're focused."
"We're relentless."
"We're confident."
"We're tough."
"We want respect."

And that was the moment we all waited for. That powerful moment finally occurred.

You see, Ravi—great players, great actors, great leaders—they all KNOW they're great. They KNOW who they are. For a team, this season, like every season, is a journey to find that out. But the quicker you can find it out, the more consistent you'll play, and the more at peace you'll play. Thus, you'll play faster and with a greater knowing.

When the word respect came up, we had a great conversation because respect is not something you can say lightly; it is a strong word. Something that people yearn for and seek out.

Tomorrow we get to show 30 million people on TV who we are. We get to show them that our practice and preparation are the real deal. We need to go do what we do, nothing special and nothing miraculous. Just do what we do.

That is why we practice; it is why you practice before an audition or show. You prepare so that when they say "showtime," it's easy.

My favorite part of Friday nights is the end. When every player or coach goes to his room, looks himself in the eye, and asks himself if he is ready, if he KNOWS.

Ravi—our players know. Our staff knows. Time to trust in our preparation. Time to enjoy the moments that this game for the ages will provide. Time to just "go play."

Time to let it rip.

Time to get that yearned-for and sought-after respect.

Love ya, man,

Yogi

DATE: September 13, 2008
SUBJECT: Re: Ohio State

Dude, I'm so excited for you today! I know you will destroy! I have a new way of thinking at auditions now.... It's not "I hope I get it" or "My voice better be on point"; it is rather "I am it" and "I am going to kill it." Whether I am right for the role or if I book it is not the important factor. And once I truly believe that, I am golden. I go in, and do my thing, and that's what's important. Now today, you go in, and do your thing, bro! I'll be watching.

-Ravi

DATE: September 13, 2008
SUBJECT: Game Day

Ravi,

It's finally Saturday. Let's freaking go, man! So jacked for this game, but now that I'm sitting in my Marriott bed at the team hotel writing this to you, I can say that a very comfortable calm has come over me this morning. A poise of some sort. I feel relaxed and focused.

I think we are going to crush these guys. I think we will seriously blow them out.

I think we're going to make them look normal…in an uncommonly common fashion.

We'll see.

Enjoy the game, bro.

Love ya,

Yogi

DATE: September 14, 2008
SUBJECT: Post-Game

Ravi,

So we beat them 35-3 and it wasn't even close. Honestly, we should have put up 50 on them. The atmosphere was incredible, and the boys were raring to go. The sidelines were nuts as celebrities came out from everywhere to be a part of the Trojans and our game.

Pre-game was almost funny. As I was cruising up the tunnel toward the locker room, for our final pre-game meeting, I began to notice all of the people "outside" of our program. By "outside" I mean those who are not coaches, players, or support staff. Those outsiders were so serious and so nervous. I swear it was like they were going to play the game! They were staring straight ahead, faces stone cold, and when I would smile at them, it was as though I had just committed a felony. I mean, "Hey, dude, relax. All we need from you is to talk trash to the Buckeyes and have a few Cokes on ice for us after the game."

Players and coaches were actually more relaxed than one could imagine. Our preparation truly set us free and our mindset was to ENJOY the moment, not stress about it because there was nothing more we could do other than play. And play is exactly what our boys did. No one played great; there were no superhuman efforts, and we did not draw up any new plays in the dirt. We just did what we did. We just executed what we practiced. We really…just let it rip and had a blast doing it.

And Mom and Dad got to watch. What better day could I ask for?

And yes, afterwards, we celebrated into the night.

And now, on the morning after, my head hurts, Mom is jacked about going for a run on the infamous sand dunes, and Oregon State is next. Rock on, brother!

Miss ya,

Yogi

"CHANGE IS COMING"

26

DATE: September 17, 2008
SUBJECT: The Streets

Ravi,

Yesterday to celebrate Coach Carroll's birthday, we headed into the streets of Los Angeles to finish a piece for *60 Minutes*. The feature on Coach Carroll is going to be amazing as the crew has filmed us for seven days, including the LA LIVEPEACE 08 rally, the 1-on-1 interview, the Ohio State game, the post-game locker room, the follow-up interview, a night in the streets, and today's finale with Coach being mic'd up at practice.

I need to tell you about what happened last night when we went into the streets. First of all, let me get you up to speed. Randomly during the off-season, and about twice during the season, Coach goes into the streets of Los Angeles to talk to people in neighborhoods where gang violence is prevalent. There he talks to kids, current gang members, former gang members, and peacekeepers. He walks into the most dangerous areas of LA, such as Watts, Nickerson Gardens, Grape Streets, and throughout South Central. But he walks into these areas as not only a coach, but also a friend.

After our Rose Bowl win over Illinois last year, Coach and I talked about what I would do for the upcoming season. Would I stay, would I leave, would I move on? I told him that if I did come back, he would have to take me into the streets with him as the inner workings of those communities have always interested me. So, finally, after about eight months, he took me along.

As we entered Nickerson Gardens, a community center in the heart of gang territory, I actually felt relaxed. I mean, after being in the West Bank and third-world countries, I was not worried, as I have learned that I cannot control what might occur.

Outside of a gymnasium, Coach spoke with a few of the children. It was one of the most amazing moments of my life. Not because the children's comments opened up my eyes to life on the streets, but because Coach Carroll's actions proved how easy it is to aid people who are just looking for a chance. How, you ask?

It was simple—he just listened to those kids.

As I sat back and watched Coach listen to the kids, young adults, and older adults speak about their life and community, it was as impressive as anything I've seen him do (which includes winning games and giving great speeches). And after listening, he didn't offer the greatest speech of all time, but rather he offered them optimism and friendship.

One thing that one of the children said struck a chord for me. "I go to school from 8-3. What am I supposed to do after that? OK, I go to the community center from 3-10. What am I supposed to do after that? Gang violence is everywhere, at every turn and at every corner. I mean, I go to these centers and I meet a Mexican kid who's cool and we become friends, but what happens when I'm with my crew and he's with his and we run into each other and a fight breaks out? Am I supposed to back him up and bail on my boys who I live next to, or do I jump in with my boys and ruin the friendship and peace I had with my new Latino friend? We can't win, man. The gang life is everywhere."

Then one of the guys with us spoke up. "Son, you just have to keep believing. Change is coming. It's about to happen."

The young boy responded with, "Change is coming….I've been hearing that for years and there ain't no change. When's it coming, man?"

My heart dropped, but that is when Coach picked those kids back up. "Look guys, you have to keep competing. We know it won't be easy; it's not supposed to be. But right now, right here, you are living that change, and it is up to you, to keep competing, because I can't do anything. Every day, every hour, every moment, you have to compete to live your life with peace."

And for the first time, those young teens smiled.

After about an hour of watching Coach, I decided to start talking to some of the people at the community center, and it was a blast. Before I knew it, we were playing hoops in the gym, and after about ten minutes, Coach Carroll, Byron Pitts (the journalist doing the story), and the rest of the kids were hoopin'. And of course, Coach made the game-winning shot.

From there, we went to Grape Streets, where the projects look like a prison. Each apartment is identical in color and size; the only way to differentiate them is by the number on the building.

There we met with young men who had left gang life.

Once again, we listened.

We listened to their newfound approach to life. We listened to their upstart music careers as they rapped for us. We listened to how they plan on educating kids to steer clear of gangs. We also listened to how they are going to change their community from within, one person at a time.

Only an hour earlier we had heard a 15-year-old say that every night before bed, he pictures himself in a coffin, and now a 30-year-old with a son was speaking of how life is full of opportunity. A perplexing moment for me. The younger kid should have been dreaming about making the NFL, going to college, or becoming the next president, but it was the elder statesmen, the former gang member, the person who did time who was dreaming.

The best part of the night came at the end when Byron Pitts spoke to Coach. "Let me ask you a question. It's 1:30 AM, you're the top coach in the country, can do anything in this city, yet you choose to be in South Central and Watts at 1:30 in the morning...on your birthday.... What is wrong with you?"

Pete's answer was classic. "I dunno, man.... I like to be here. I want to be here."

Today, those same young kids and a few of the young adults came to practice. They had smiles on their faces, were tossing the ball around, and for a few moments, they saw hope and believed in change.

And as I write you this long e-mail, I can only think that it is our duty to continue to give them that hope and to create that change that has been promised for so long.

Our greatest gift is that we control ourselves. You, Ravi, control the power of you. For instance, when you wake up, you decide if you're going to be in a good mood or not; when I wake up I decide if I'm going to be an jerk to the players I coach. So if we can control our minds and put ourselves in a positive mindset, then imagine if we spread that positive approach to our buddy...and he passes it to his buddy...and so on. I mean, imagine a world where the simple philosophy each and every day is, "Be nice" or "Don't kill someone today." I mean, imagine that!

We, as two kids with great upbringings, have the ability to change those around us, and it is our duty to do so. And if you don't agree, just ask the 15-year-old who has been waiting on change for years. He has to walk home every night knowing that he may get killed, and instead of dreaming about being on Broadway or coaching on the Coliseum floor, he is imagining himself in an oak coffin, seven feet under the very ground we walk on.

Change needs to come, and we are the ones who can bring it.

Love ya, pal,

Yogi

_____

DATE: September 18, 2008
SUBJECT: Graduation

Ravi,

Tonight I went to the first graduation of gang interventionists. It was sponsored by "A Better LA," Coach Carroll's foundation. An awesome event as I got to see some of the people I saw in the streets a few nights ago. While the graduation was not very exciting, the graduates were definitely impressive.

50 people from seventeen communities received their peacekeeping degrees. In a 6-month course, the students underwent mental, physical, and social challenges. They took exams. They had to prove that they could learn not only how to protect the streets of their communities but also how to sit in a room with one another.

Why, you ask? Well, many of these people are from rival gangs, and a few years ago, it was not uncommon for one member of this actual class to try to kill another member. As you might imagine, the anger and tension in the first few classes was palpable. But the leader, Aquil Basheer, taught them how to co-exist, how to learn together, and how to change views that they had held onto for such a long time.

Unreal, man….It was just so powerful.

I'm out. Got a date in a few.

Yogi

OREGON STATE

27

DATE: September 20, 2008
SUBJECT: 27 Years Old

Hey man,

Thanks for the call today on my birthday. Hard to believe, huh?

Surfed all day today as the waves were about 6 foot. Got in the green room on my first wave. It was awesome. Anyway, I'm out. Work tomorrow, bro. Gotta beat the Beavers! Pac-10 opener!

Yogi

P.S. When are you setting me up with one of your actress friends?

DATE: September 22, 2008
SUBJECT: GA's

Ravi,

Hope work is going well. Don't worry, man, something will turn up. Keep working hard, bro, and remember: 1) Good things happen to good people and 2) Hard work always pays off.

We play on a Thursday night this week, which is awesome. I love Thursday night ball as the entire nation is watching and we get to put on a show. They beat us last time we went up to Corvallis, so it should be an interesting game. They are not very complicated, but play a physical style of defense that will force us to execute. Which I fully expect us to do.

I have a ton to do tonight to get ready, so I'm out, bro.

Yogi

DATE: September 23, 2008
SUBJECT: Joe #4

Hey, man,

Had my 4th cup of joe today.

Yogi

DATE: September 24, 2008
SUBJECT: Oregon State – Friday Night (Wednesday Night)

Ravi,

Tomorrow is the third of our three openers. UVA was the season opener, Ohio State was the home opener, and Oregon State is the Pac-10 opener. While most of the college football world will not agree, tomorrow is the most important game of the three. Obviously because it's the next one, but also because all we can control is our conference, and this is our conference opener.

Anyway, tomorrow will be awesome, as we get to prove to the nation that we are not like most teams who falter after a big game. We are uncommon. To be honest, there were zero signs of our taking these guys lightly this week. We should roll and play sharp, fast, and, most important—physical.

Hope you get to watch, and the Trojans are about to rip!

Love ya, man,

Yogi

DATE: September 26, 2008
SUBJECT: Angry

Ravi,

So we just got upset today, or I guess yesterday, as it's 3:30 AM and I'm sitting on my couch. I have never been this angry about a loss. Usually, I'm upset, pissed off, or just in a bad mood…but I'm really angry, man. I've always said, "You show me a good loser and I'll show you a permanent one," and as I sit here, I am just…well, angry.

We lost 27-21. Basically just got the shit beat out of us. Seriously, they just beat us up on both lines of scrimmage, and we couldn't do anything about it. Our field position sucked and we only ran 21 plays on offense in the first half. Our game plan was awesome on offense and defense, but we missed tackles, got dumb penalties, and never got into a groove.

Down 21-0 at the half, we came out roaring and scored on our first two drives of the third quarter, and I thought we were rolling. We then stalled a bit, got a bunch of penalties, and before we knew it, the game was over, their fans were storming the field, and Erin Andrews was interviewing Mike Riley, the Beavers head coach.

I can't even turn on ESPN as I think I'm going to throw up if I see one highlight.

But as bad as this night was, I did hear the great news! Congrats on being named full-time to the cast of *Altar Boyz*!!! That is huge, man, as I know you have wanted this. And to have a show in NYC is awesome, as you will only keep succeeding!!!

So proud of you, man, as your approach has obviously paid off.

Love ya and miss ya, man,

Yogi

DATE: September 26, 2008
SUBJECT: 4:30 AM…Still Angry

We lost. We lost. We f-ing lost!

I still cannot believe that it actually happened. We lost to Oregon State 27-21. They beat the shit out of us on both lines of scrimmage and we ran only 51 plays. Unreal, man!

Talk about a sick feeling.

And you know what the ironic part is? Remember when I told you about how serious the "outsiders" were before games and how relaxed we were? Well, after the game, another notable moment occurred. As I walked out of the locker room, the fact that we lost really hit me. I then looked around at our players, and they too were upset. But they also got over it quickly.

There, in freaking Corvallis, was where I really noticed how hard coaches take losses and how everything we do during the week—all of the film-watching, play-drawing, and note-writing—is all for the 60 minutes on gameday. And that our love for this game is unmatched by most.

Now, I'm not mad that some of our players got over the loss quickly. In fact, I want them to do that since harboring the loss does nothing positive for them.

But the losses are what haunt you as a coach, what make you want to throw up, what tear your insides out, and what can ruin your life.

So, as the sun is rising in Hermosa Beach, the happiest place on earth, every member of our staff is likely still awake. Some watching the TV copy on their DVR, some having a few beers, some just sitting on their couches staring, or some writing an e-mail to their younger brother. Regardless, we are all in a state of shock, disbelief, and nausea.

But, as you hopefully know, we will not just bounce back: we will roar back.

I wish we were playing Oregon tomorrow.

Miss ya, bro,

Yogi

DATE: September 26, 2008
SUBJECT: 5:00 AM…R U serious

Bro,

Last thing before I go to bed. How about this—someone told me after the game to be a good loser. Screw that!

Like I've always told you, "You show me a good loser, and I'll show you a permanent one."

Yogi

DATE: September 26, 2008
SUBJECT: Byron Pitts

Ravi,

So I did laundry, cleaned the apartment, and worked out, and I'm not as angry as I was earlier.

Anyway, I wanted to share this with you. Byron Pitts, a great friend of mine and reporter for *60 Minutes* and CBS, wrote this to me today.

> *Yogi,*
>
> *Watched the game last night. Not the outcome any of us wanted, but so what? What I found was awesome: EVERYTIME the camera cut to you on the sideline talking to Sanchez…u were smiling…looked to be speaking words of encouragement and strength and knowledge into your young quarterback's ear. THAT'S LEADERSHIP!*
>
> *EVERYTIME I saw Coach…sometimes intensely focused…sometimes perplexed… sometimes seeming to say 'almost'—but never once did he look discouraged.*
>
> *THAT'S A TESTIMONY.*
>
> *I know you guys don't consider yourselves particularly religious…but I watched both of you and saw God. His grace. His strength.*
>
> *Proud of you, my friend. I believe I'm getting it now: WIN FOREVER has next to nothing to do with a score. It's bigger. It's longer lasting. It's more important. What those young men saw directly and indirectly from you and Coach Thursday in Oregon are lessons that will last longer than the hurt of one loss or memories of the exact score. You both lived your testimony—No matter what…men stand up, stay positive…stay believing.*
>
> *Dr. King once said, and my mom often repeats, "A man can't stand on your neck if you're holding your head up."*
>
> *Bless you, my friend. Please know you're in my prayers. Same with Coach. Things on this end are well. Joyce and Cathy tell me the tape looks great. Great energy and passion. We'll find the truth in all that videotape and interviews and we will tell it.*
>
> *Please give me your parents' address…and a home address for Coach if you have it. I'm old- school…I prefer hand-written notes to e-mail.*
>
> *Godspeed, my friend. Still thinking and praying over our last conversation.*

Best

B

Byron is one of the three most impressive people I've ever met. A great friend, an honorable man, and someone who makes this world a better place.

He is a storyteller, Ravi. A man who changes the world through his voice, his eyes, and his soul.

And, in my opinion, he accomplishes all of those because he does one thing extremely well. Like our good friend Santiago, he listens to his heart.

I can't wait until you meet him, as he lives in the city. I'll see if he wants to see your show.

Miss ya, man.

Love ya,

Yogi

DATE: September 27, 2008
SUBJECT: First Debate

Hey man,

Sitting here watching mindless TV, otherwise known as VH1, which I secretly love….

Am still dealing with the loss, but after watching McCain and Obama go after it tonight, I think I'm over our last game.

Not sure if you had a chance to watch the debate, but it was a blast. Going into it McCain was expected to beat Obama easily as this debate discussed foreign policy, but Obama not only held his own, he also took a few shots at McCain.

While what they discussed is obviously huge, what was most impressive was the strategy behind Obama's approach. He was the aggressor.

On the biggest night of his political career, he attacked. He was aggressive, focused, and poised. He didn't wait to see what his opponent would do. It was like he didn't even care because he KNEW who he was and what he stood for. Sure, there were moments when McCain pissed Obama off, got under his skin, and annoyed him, but he never let it get to him, or at least never showed it. You see, that is the power of poise—never letting your opponent know what you are thinking, never letting him know that he got you, never losing sight of the ultimate goal.

It sounds like Barack took some advice from a kid I know who just booked a huge gig in the City that Doesn't Sleep. He didn't back down, he stayed true to who he is, and he had a quiet confidence that bordered on arrogance.

Lastly, and almost most importantly, Obama respected his opponent, he respected his predecessors, he respected his profession, he respected the event, he respected his audience, and he respected the nation he will soon serve as Commander in Chief. And like that kid I know who lives in NYC, he listened to his heart and let it rip.

Congratulations on your new gig and keep pushing forward as you set a new normal for yourself and your career.

It's like Dad has always said, "To thine own self be true…."

Your biggest fan,

Yogi Roth

P.S. You should be proud of yourself, pal.

OREGON DUCKS

28

DATE: October 1, 2008
SUBJECT: Joe #5 & #6

Needed 2 cups to get through today. Losing sucks.

Yogi

DATE: October 2, 2008
SUBJECT: Only a Game

Ravi,

Thanks for the call last night, appreciate it. It's so funny that this recent loss has affected us as a staff so much. I mean, it has not left the pits of our stomachs. The players, they should be over it; 20-year-olds can move on quickly. But while we've had a great week of practice and the mood has been very upbeat, our staff is still sick when we think about the Oregon State game.

Not sure how much ball you watch, but I get to watch a ton of it in my spare time. For instance, Pitt just beat South Florida, who was ranked #10 in the nation. A great win for Pitt, but those coaches at South Florida are miserable right now. And it's just football; it's only a game!

But this game, Ravi, like your shows, is our life. We live and die with each moment, each snap, and each game, like you live and die with each line, each scene, and each performance.

And while we get to be re-born with every new game or every new performance, that sole fact of how much a pass play or a scene means to us proves that we love what we do. Because, for the time, effort, and heart we pour into our professions, we better love it.

And that love is what will allow you to be the best actor New York City has ever seen, and that love of the game will allow the Trojans to kick Oregon's ass this weekend.

A buddy in town, so I'm off. Talk to you later.

Yogi

DATE: October 3, 2008
SUBJECT: Friday Night

Ravi,

So it's Friday night! You know this is my favorite night, and boy, was this one to remember. I think we turned our season around tonight. I think we just began what will be a march toward a championship. I think we are going to actualize our potential tomorrow night, and the Oregon Ducks will be the ones who have to deal with it.

On offense, we need to do 4 things:

1) Protect the football.
2) Be physical.
3) Play fast.
4) Dig down and find out whatever it takes to win and call on that. Find out if we have it in us to give up our personal stuff for the common goal of winning. Because, Ravi, that is what we do around here….We win. As you know, losing is never accepted.

When Coach Carroll addressed the team tonight it was phenomenal. He began talking to them about what a "teachable moment" is. Because we, the coaches, are essentially teachers. We teach how to block, tackle, throw, and catch. Tonight he brought up one of our captains, Jeff Byers, to teach the players a lesson. Jeff is a 5th-year senior and one of the best kids on the team. He is not only starting at left guard but also getting his MBA at USC's prestigious Marshall Business School. So Jeff taught the boys about the financial crisis our nation is in right now. He talked of the $700 billion bailout that the government is proposing and how our nation got so indebted. A great lesson, as most players and probably most coaches didn't know the details regarding our economy. (Dad would love to have been in this meeting.)

After Jeff's "teachable moment," Coach made sure to follow up with his own "teachable moment."

And that is when our season turned around.

He spoke of what it means to play at USC and in the Coliseum. You see, Ravi, in the last 6 years, we have lost only once. And that was my fault vs. Stanford. (Remember, the QB broke his finger and we kept him in.)

Anyway, we reminded our players that we have dominated at the Los Angeles Memorial Coliseum.

None of the great teams—the Yankees, the Bulls, the Patriots, Brazil's soccer team—have EVER accomplished what we have in our home venue. To lose only once—once—on your home turf in six seasons is unheard of. And we had to remind our players what that meant.

Members of our staff spoke.

First it was Sark:
"You work out over 250 times at 6:00 AM for 6 chances at the Coliseum. Our staff works 16-hour days for 6 chances at the Coliseum. The SC interlock does not allow you to win, does not just make it happen on Saturday.... Your hard work and dedication to this process are what allow us to dominate at home. We develop a belief through our hard work and earn the right to wear the Cardinal and Gold. Only 5 trips left.... What are you gonna do?"

Then Kris Richard, a current coach and former Trojan:
"The spirit of Troy is for real. The ground you play on is sacred. The ones who have been there before, the legends, would never take it for granted and neither must you. When we chant 'War Time' while interlocking our arms, it is for real. Do not let it pass you by. Respect the floor of the Coliseum because that is where greatness lies."

Ken Norton, Jr.:
"As a player at UCLA, I can remember every time I got to play at the Coliseum. I remember every tackle, every missed tackle, every moment. From sitting at my stall before the game to walking down the tunnel, I can still feel it. You see, as a player and as a team, you must stand for something. If you don't, then you've got nothing. We've got to stand for the Coliseum. In Dallas, we stood for our stadium. I can remember one year when the 49ers came to town. Three days before the game, we decided that we weren't even going to let them stand on our field. We wouldn't even let them stand on it! So when they did, when they came out of that tunnel

in pre-game warm-ups, we kicked their ass. We got in a fight right there! And at that moment, we knew we had them beat. When an opponent comes into your house, they are trying to invade you, and being invaded is the last thing you want. The Coliseum is what we stand for."

Rocky Seto:
"Tomorrow will be my 103rd time at the Coliseum, first as a player and then as a coach. I feel it is my duty to count my blessings and I do so every time we enter the Coliseum. I met with Troy Polamalu before the Virginia game and he told me about the USC contingency in the NFL and how they always reminisce about their days on the Coliseum floor. I asked Troy if he would give up his Super Bowl ring to play one more time at the Coliseum. His response: 'I ponder that thought often.' That is how powerful playing at the Coliseum is."

Todd McNair:
"Those who have set the bar in the past 6 years are those who 'respect' the game. They 're- spect' those who played before them. They 'respect' the greatness that lives on that hallowed ground. That 'respect' is why they've won."

Pat Ruel:
"I was shocked my first time in the Coliseum. I looked around the locker room and noticed how there were no names on the backs of our jerseys. I then went out and watched us play and realized that we were 1 heartbeat, 1 mind, 1 soul. I realized that to be a Trojan is an honor and to be able to showcase that pride and love of the game at the Coliseum is something I would do for free for the rest of my life."

Then Coach Carroll reminded the players that when they can learn from a "teachable moment" and when they can connect to the Coliseum and what it represents, that is when they will play so fast, so hard, and with such passion that it will never matter who the person is lining up across the ball.

As this was going on I thought of two things:

1) Going into the streets with Coach a few weeks ago, when the teenagers and young adults spoke of the Trojans and the Coliseum with such pride. You see, Ravi, out here, like everywhere, people go through difficulties, whether fam- ily problems, relationship issues, drug addiction, gang violence, etc. But in the streets of LA, in the heart of LA, the Coliseum is one of those places where everyone can forget the problems in their lives and come together for 60 minutes of football 6 times a year on Saturday afternoons.

It is a powerful thought. From the Olympics to JFK announcing his presidential candidacy, from the Raiders and Rams to the Trojans—the Coliseum is history. But even more important, the Coliseum is Los Angeles and all it represents.

2) The sacrifice that our entire team and staff put forth. From the workouts to the film room to last-minute preparations, I am so proud.

What we do is special because it is more than football. It is about influencing and changing a society, and we get to do that in one of the coolest and most historic venues in the world.

Tomorrow, at 5:12 PM, the Trojans get to walk down the tunnel at the Los Angeles Memorial Coliseum one more time. Tomorrow, at 5:12 PM, the Trojans get to show who we are. Tomorrow, at 5:12 PM, the Trojans will begin a march toward the end of a long season.

Tomorrow…we let it rip.

Hope you get to watch.

Love ya, bro,

Yogi

ARIZONA STATE

29

DATE: October 5, 2008
SUBJECT: Win but a HUGE loss

Ravi,

So we beat the Oregon Ducks 44-10. From running 54 plays a week earlier, we ran 75 against the Ducks. The Coliseum was rocking and the boys played their tails off. The emotion, energy, and overall feel were exactly what it was supposed to be for a game at the Coli. The boys heeded what was said the night before the game.

BUT…our starting quarterback, our leader, our potential Heisman, got hurt. Mark Sanchez got sacked and it was ugly. Thankfully, his brace saved his knee, and he was diagnosed with a bone bruise.

When our backup, Mitch Mustain, went into the game, he actually did a solid job and even got to throw a touchdown. As of now, Mark is out for the game, and Mitch is going to have to start against a very good ASU squad. I guess we'll find out if I can coach at all as our back-up may have to lead the Trojans.

I think it'll be a long week in the office.

Yogi

DATE: October 7, 2008
SUBJECT: Mitch

Hey man,

Mitch had a decent practice today, and I think we'll be OK. If not, I may have to move to NYC and live with you, as I should be fired if he plays poorly.

Yogi

DATE: October 8, 2008
SUBJECT: Mark

This is a classic week. Mark practiced today and looked good. So, we are developing two game plans: one for Mitch and another for Mark. But, let me tell you, doing that is miserable.

Long hours in this profession are natural and expected, but when you are doing two game plans it is not ideal. Tonight is the night I prepare the wristbands for the QBs, but our call sheet is wild since we have stuff for both guys. I don't want to put plays on the wristband for Mark if he isn't going to play, as it only takes up space for Mitch, and vice versa. I thought I would get out of here at 10:00 PM and it's 12:15 AM.

It is interesting to watch as guys get thrust into the spotlight. Mitch is preparing as the starter and just left the office after he and I studied all night. On the one hand, I'm so proud of him and the time he is putting in. On the other, it proves that we can always work harder, since he never prepared this much before. Funny how human nature works.

As it relates to acting, I wonder if you prepare differently for a show like Altar Boyz, where you are the lead, versus a smaller role that you had on As the World Turns?

Anyway, we are always telling our players that there are "No Choices." Meaning you can't pick and choose when to prepare, when to play hard, when to be disciplined. You prepare great all the time, you practice and perform at your best every snap, and you do it with a constant discipline that never wavers.

Anyway, I'm heading home. Gonna call this new gal I just met. I'm sick of only talking to dudes every day.

Love ya, man,

Yogi

P.S. Maya gets here today along with a few friends from Pitt.

DATE: October 9, 2008
SUBJECT: Day Games

Ravi,

Coach Holt, our defensive coordinator, spoke today about why he loves day games. He spoke about how college football was made for Saturdays. Since we played a lot of our games on Saturdays growing up, it took me back.

I can remember being a kid and waking up on Saturday mornings. Maya would be getting ready, as she was drum major. Mom would drop me off at the high school early and I would hang out on the practice field across from the game field and just sit on that grassy knoll. As the game began, I would watch as my heroes ran around the field. During those games, all of the kids would play tackle football on the practice field, pretending to be varsity players. For whatever reason, my world would stop as the announcer, George Hayduk (my hero, since he played at Notre Dame), would say, "Touchdown Lions! Mark Kalinowski on the carry."

After the game, which the varsity would typically lose, I would always stand near the locker room. Watching them walk in with their heads down and pants bloodied, I always told myself that my team would never walk into the locker room with our heads down like that. Kind of weird to have such vivid memories from when I was only 8 years old.

After the high school day games, we would drive home and watch the end of the Notre Dame games on NBC. Tony Rice, the Rocket, Derrick Mays, and Ron Powlus were the stars I grew up with. After their games, Dad would always hang with me, and I'd ask him to throw "diver" after "diver."

Of course, each catch was the game winner.

Anyway, we play Saturday at 12:30 PM, and as my mind travels back to 1988, I can only chuckle and realize how much I love this game of football.

We're gonna beat ASU, and it looks like Mark is going to rip.

I'm out,

Yogi

DATE: October 10, 2008
SUBJECT: Friday Night

Ravi,

By now you know how awesome Friday nights are, and tonight was no different.

Sark spoke of routine—tonight renting a movie, then tomorrow showering, shaving, and showering again—all before 7:30 AM. He talked about the Trojan walk, entering the Coliseum and staring down the opponent, kicking their ass in the game, and celebrating afterwards. All in all, his best speech of the year. You really should make it one of your monologues if you ever audition for a sports piece.

Coach Carroll told the team that he feels that this night is the most critical of the year because of last week. Remember how we had to get an understanding of what it meant to play at the Coliseum last Friday night? Now we need to re-capture that emotion.

Our team now knows what it takes to play well and win and what it takes to play horribly and lose. It is up to us to capture the former and run with it.

I would assume it is like going in and doing great in an audition or being just OK. You have obviously had great auditions, but do you know why you did so well? If so, then you should be able to capture that feeling before every audition from that moment on. If you don't know why, then you are just relying on hope in each reading. And, if you are only hoping, then you are like most of our opponents.

I truly think that many teams hope that the Trojans play like poorly. They hope that we turn the ball over. They hope that we drop the ball. They hope that we blow a coverage.

On the other side, we know we will play great, we know we will protect the football, we know we will succeed.

I believe that to be great at anything, you must KNOW that you are great.

For instance, you need to KNOW that you are a great actor and then go kick ass in your audition, even if you don't get the part. Because once you know you are great, you can perform at ease and at peace.

But you need to know that the KNOWING is not an arrogance; rather, it is a confidence that borders on cockiness. That line is very fine, and it must be respected.

So how do you get to that knowing? Well, as I've learned from Coach Carroll and Pat Kirwan, you need to have a style, theme, and vision in your life. Then you must practice.

From practice, you develop a confidence that enables you to trust your preparation. That confidence and trust give you the ability to focus on the task or audition at hand. Essentially, you earn the right to know who you are by going through the process I just mentioned.

And the funny thing is, man, you don't need to do anything special to achieve this level of thinking. It's actually pretty simple. You just need to ask yourself those questions and listen to your heart as it answers them.

You are finding out who you are and becoming the best you can possibly be, Ravi. That in itself allows you to become the best actor you can be, the best waiter, the best brother, the best friend. For us tomorrow, it allows us to become the best team on the field.

Miss ya, bro,

Yogi

P.S. Look for Maya on TV—she better be cheering like crazy!

DATE: October 12, 2008
SUBJECT: 28-0

We won 28-0. It was ugly—had 4 turnovers in the 2nd half. The defense played great and the offense was sloppy. But I would rather win ugly than lose pretty.

Went out last night with Maya and my buddies and it was a blast. They think they set me up with this girl they met on Friday. She sounds cool. I'll keep you posted, but don't hold your breath.

Got to watch the film. We need to get better as we head to Washington State this week.

Yogi

Date: October 13, 2009
Subject: Re: 28-0

Yogi,

Nice win. Got to see you on the sideline after a touchdown...I think you yelled a curse...but it looked cool. Haha.

Thanks for your e-mails and sorry for the lack of responses. Have been auditioning for other shows and Altar Boyz is, as you would say, 'ripping.'

Was on the train last night coming home from the Village and was reading your e-mail and asked myself what my style was and I couldn't put it in a sentence during the entire ride, but after going to the gym today, it hit me...like your team and your quarterback, when I go to an audition I just go for it, because...well, why would I hold back?

Off to work...later.

Ravi

WASHINGTON STATE

30

DATE: October 14, 2008
SUBJECT: Mid-Season

Ravi,

There comes a point during every season where the grind hits you. Typically it's a combination of working too many consecutive 16-hour days, players aggravating you, and lack of sleep.

As a graduate assistant, I understand that the hours are a part of the job, so there's no sense in letting it get to me. But I haven't gotten any sleep in the past few weeks because people from all over the country have come to visit. The scout team is also annoying me because they are likely sick of hearing me yell at them, and we didn't play very well last week. So there you have it—the mid-season aggravation.

Now I'm just thinking about getting through the week, putting a beat down on Washington State, and going to bed.

Hope you're well.

Yogi

DATE: October 15, 2008
SUBJECT: Recruiting Meetings

So we have these recruiting meetings every Wednesday morning. I would guess that they are different from most recruiting meetings around the country. As we evaluate the best players in America, a mix of T.I., Lil' Wayne, Bon Jovi, and Metallica plays in the background.

Around a long brown table sit our staff members evaluating film, eating Denny's, bobbing our heads to the beat, and cracking one-liners as we start our Wednesday.

All in all, even though I'm still tired, I do have the best job in the world.

Love ya, man,

Yogi

DATE: October 17, 2008
SUBJECT: Call Sheets

While I could write an entire book on this subject, this e-mail will have to suffice. I'm writing it on the plane as we head to Pullman, Washington. You see, we too have scripts. They are 2-sided, legal-sized pieces of cardboard separated by lines (both dotted and solid), colors, and segments, such as 3rd Down and 4-6, Rip-It Zone (Red Zone), and F.T.S. (which means Feed The Stud).

Each sheet is built from the ground up each week by our offensive staff and monitored by Coach Sark, Johnny Mo, and me. We type, correct, shred, and type again.

At the end of each week, when it is finalized, Justin Mesa and I go over it one final time in a completely anal fashion. When we are finished, we print out about 11 copies and take them to our laboratory.

Here we serve as the doctors of the call sheets. Really we just laminate them, but doctors of the call sheets sounds way cooler. Because it is not just ordinary lamination. We slide every call sheet through the laminating machine with poise and grace. After the first 7 are done, we take a moment, gather ourselves, and begin the final process, which we've dubbed "the delivering of the baby."

That "baby" is, of course, Sark's call sheet. And we laminate 4 of them for him each week. Obviously, he can use only one, but like many play callers, he needs to feel comfortable with his call sheet. And he feels comfortable when he has a call sheet that is firm, strong, and stable. Just as many A-list actors want their green room a certain way, our A-list coach wants his call sheet a certain way.

As stupid as that sounds, I like it. It proves to me the importance of detail, and Justin and I actually take great pride in laminating a "stiff" call sheet.

This process has been going on for a few years now, and throughout it, we have recruited such helpers as Al, Jared, Randall, and various student workers. Justin always washes his hands prior to the "birth," and we use clips to pin down each side of the call sheet as it pops through the laminator to ensure that it is sealed tightly. We need the clips because to make the call sheet stiff, we need to slide anywhere from 2-5 sheets of cardstock in between the front and back of the call sheet.

All in all, Fridays in our office are often comical, sometimes ridiculous, and always detail-oriented. But details are important, and I'm proud of our goal to "do it better than it has ever been done before"…even if that means being an anal graduate assistant.

Talk later, man,

Yogi

Date: October 17, 2008
Subject: Friday Night

Offensively we need to do 6 things to win tomorrow:

1) Protect the football. To do that, all personal gain must be sacrificed.
2) Be physical.
3) Play fast. We are better than the Cougars and should prove it by playing fast.
4) Play with urgency. Play as though our balls are on the line from the 1st snap (and we are currently in 4th place in the Pac-10).
5) Play as a team. Play for one another and be proud of that.
6) Get our rest. We are all a little tired and it's a 12:30 game.

As Coach Carroll addressed the team, he brought a unique energy to the meeting. He is jacked for the game because it is a great opportunity for our players to prove that we love this sport. It was so easy to feel him tonight: he is completely correct that it doesn't matter who or where we play. We just go ball-out and dominate, regardless of the opponent. And to do that, we don't need to do anything special. We just need to be us, play how we practice, and prove our respect for this game.

Reporters asked us all week how we get our boys fired up for this game considering

Washington State is horrible. The answer: "We are always fired up!"

Ravi—this is a direct parallel to acting, auditioning, and performing. You never act differently. You never adjust your lines if a big-time producer is in the seats or no one is there to watch you. There are No Choices! You perform to the best of your ability every time out on that stage, and that is more than enough.

I know you are aware of that, but you may not be aware of the other side. When the stakes are higher, competitors in both of our professions think they need to try harder or do something out of the ordinary. In fact, though, both our team and your acting are already out of the ordinary due to the way we prepare and practice. Settling for average or trying to be special is what losers do because they never had an identity in the first place.

I'm out. Need some rest,

Yogi

Date: October 18, 2008
Subject: 69-0

Ravi,

On plane back to LA sitting next to BC, who is asleep. We beat Washington State 69-0 today, and it wasn't even hard. Just like I wrote to you last night, we went out and played how we know how to play. Protecting the football, being physical, playing fast, playing urgently, and playing as a team, we dominated every phase and did what we were supposed to do.

It's Arizona next week at 7:00 PM in their stadium. Tucson is a wild place to play, and their fans will be jacked. But for now, it's time for a nap and maybe a relaxing night at my apartment.

Love ya and miss ya, bro,

Yogi

P.S. Then again, I might have to see what is happening in Hermosa tonight and celebrate.... sleep is over-rated anyway.

P.S.S. Keep doing great in your shows! I'll get out to see one as soon as I can!

UNIVERSITY OF ARIZONA

31

DATE: October 22, 2008
SUBJECT: Signals

Ravi,

So every Wednesday night I sit at Sark's computer and make the wristbands for our games. Our QB reads the plays off the wristbands. It is my job to coordinate the wristbands and Sark's call sheet. There are a color and number for each play on the wristband, and a strategy that comes with that.

For instance, if our opponent is watching me signal and can tell that when I touch my head it's a run, or when I touch my leg it's a pass, we're in trouble. Thus, every Wednesday night, when everyone has left the office, I sit at Sark's desk with two computers, one with the master call sheet pulled up on screen and the other with my wristband document. Here is where I get to compete.

I compete with the opponent as I play a little game in my head. I use past wristbands to figure out my tendencies and try to stay one step ahead of the other team's defensive coordinator. We've already established that I'm pathetic and, yes, I know, take the wristbands way too seriously. But I think that little battles like this matter.

Love ya,

Yogi

DATE: October 24, 2008
SUBJECT: A long week

Ravi,

Not gonna lie: I slacked this week on the e-mails. Have been tied up, tired, and working on the call sheet. This is the third week in a row where our call sheet has been manipulated and altered during the week. One of our receivers might not play, thus, I have to vary the personnel on every play.

So today, Johnny Morton, our passing game coordinator, and I went through each play and typed in who would play depending on whether our receiver is healthy or injured. A tedious job, but it proves that details are what separate the great ones from good ones. The only issue is that I have this headache that won't quit because I went out last night and had one too many sodas.

Hope you're doing great, man…. I'm having a blast, easily more fun than any season.

Love ya,

Yogi

DATE: October 26, 2008
SUBJECT: I hate our players

We won 17-10. It was ugly. Our offense made countless mistakes. The guys I coach did not play as well as they should. It's 4:13 AM and I can say that I hate our players right now.

We need to remember that this game is easy and that to play well, you do not always need to create great plays. Sometimes you just have to let the game come to you. Like your script lines, you can't make them dramatic or emotional or funny…. You have to let that come to you naturally. It's why there is no one scene that is exactly the same, right? Because they can't be exactly the same, ever! Similar, yes; identical, no. The same in football. Just let the game come to you, and you will be able to play more clearly, more focused, and much sharper.

Regardless, after a sloppy performance, we are 6-1 heading into the final six weeks of the season without having to leave California. Up next are Washington, Cal, Stanford, Notre Dame, and UCLA, with Stanford and UCLA being the only road games.

Thankfully we won, thankfully we can learn from this, and thankfully I can go to sleep tonight.

Love ya, bro,

Yogi

P.S. I really don't hate them, but they did aggravate us tonight.

_____

DATE: October 26, 2008
SUBJECT: Football is Life

Ravi,

You know that football is your life when you come home from a game at 2:30 in the morning, eat Pop Tarts, and watch TV until 4:30 AM, and wake up at 7:00 AM just because your internal clock goes off, only to fall back asleep and dream that you are making out with a random girl in your passing game coordinator's office. In this dream, your passing game coordinator walks in on you and the gal, who happens to be his children's babysitter, and you tell him that you are there because you had to make corrections to the pass sheet that you have been working on all week.

That is when you know football is your life...or that it's mid-season.

Gotta love it, man!

Yogi

University of Washington

32

DATE: October 27, 2008
SUBJECT: Tyrone Willingham

Tyrone Willingham, the head coach at Washington, resigned today, effective at the end of the season. They are 0-8 heading into our game—a situation I would never wish upon anyone.

They lost their best player to an injury, and maybe the best player in the conference, in their QB, Jake Locker. From that point on, things went downhill for the Huskies.

Something that really bothers me when a coach resigns, or basically gets fired, is that no one ever talks about the assistant coaches who also get let go. The head coach, the man whose name gets rubbed in the mud, has to deal with a ton of scrutiny, but at least he gets paid. The assistants don't get paid (as they are typically on 1-year contacts), and it is as hard to get a job as an assistant coach at a major D-I school as it is to get a role on Broadway.

Anyway, back to work, as these guys are not as bad as you may think. Actually, their defensive coordinator, Ed Donatell, used to work with Coach Carroll and is a great coach. And as you often remind me, we did lose to Stanford last year.

I'm out,

Yogi

Date: October 29, 2008
Subject: Who Are You?

Just got done meeting with Mark Sanchez, our QB. The past few weeks he has been playing well, but very inconsistent in terms of handling his emotions. Instead of letting bad plays go, he harbors them. For instance, last week at Arizona, he threw a bad pass on the first play of the game, and he held onto that play for the remainder of the evening. And he played poorly.

So tonight I thought I would try an exercise with him. I asked him, "Mark, who are you as a quarterback?" After pondering the question, he said, "Well, I play with emotion…. I'm accurate…."

I stopped him and asked him to tell me the first thing that popped into his head. Almost under his breath, he said, "Well…a winner."

At that moment, for the first time in his life, he said out loud who he was as a QB. He made an affirmation that may change the way he looks at life, and how he perceives himself.

After he said who he was we talked about it, and I told him that he can't choose when he's a "winner" and when he's not. Winning must carry over to everything in life.

You see, Ravi, on the field, a winner would never harbor a play; he would just move to the next one. On the field, a winner would not let a mistake bring his game down; he would learn from it. On the field, a winner would never hope that he would lead his team to a victory; he would **know** that he and his team would play well and win.

Off the field, a winner would stay out of trouble. Off the field, a winner would go to class. Off the field, a winner would respect everyone.

The point is that once you make the statement about who you are, there are no times when you can or can't be that person. If that is truly **who you are**, then it is embodied in everything you do.

As Mark was about to leave, I took a line from our friend Santiago as I asked him where he got his answer. He stopped at the door, looked back, and couldn't figure it out.

And then I told him that he just listened to the one thing that would never lie to him—his heart.

Tune in this weekend to see if the player with the most emotion plays like the person he knows he is. My bet is on Mark as he is special.

Love ya, man,

Yogi

DATE: October 30, 2008
SUBJECT: Will Ferrell

Ravi,

You would have loved it today. After practice Coach Carroll played a prank on the players. A stuntman fell out of the camera lift, only to land into the arms of "Captain Compete," a superhero played by Will Ferrell. He carried him to the players and gave a speech on how "Captain Compete" was here to save Halloween.

Just as he was giving his speech, another stuntman caught on fire and "Captain Compete" ran around to grab some water to put out the fire. It was absolutely classic: as the players were caught off guard and laughed their tails off.

Check out the video on www.uscripsit.com when you can.

Yogi

DATE: October 31, 2008
SUBJECT: Friday Night and Win Forever

Halloween tonight—and in Hollywood, this day is huge. But I'm sitting in the Marriott about to fall asleep at 10:39 PM. I know, I know, I should be out, but I need some sleep.

Regardless, you need to know that this is the greatest day of the year for two reasons. One, it is the only day where a girl can, and likely will, wear anything she wants and look phenomenal. Two, this great holiday lasts for 3 days. Tomorrow, I will be celebrating not only our win, but also Halloween.

Tonight was a very important Friday night meeting as Coach Carroll talked about the concept of *Win Forever*. It began when he was a young head coach with the New York Jets, in his very first game against the Buffalo Bills. Long after the game, which the Jets won, he walked back into the Bills stadium to get a look at the field once more, as it went from a sold out stadium to one relatively empty. There, he noticed all of the conference championship banners. It was then that he understood that being a true champion did not mean winning the Super Bowl one year, but winning your conference title year after year. And the only way to do that is to always compete, day in and day out, in everything you do. Simply said, you're either competing or you're not. Or if you want to *Win Forever, Always Compete*.

And that is easily applied to you bro. As an actor, you're either competing or you're not. And to compete at the highest level, you must prepare at the highest level every chance you get.

This is not an easy thing to do. It takes commitment and focus, and the question looms over you of how far do you want to take your career. Or, in our case, how far do we want to take our team. I think the answer for both of us is that we want to take it as far as we can. We want to *Win Forever*.

I'm out, bro,

Yogi

DATE: November 2, 2008
SUBJECT: 56-0

We beat them 56-0 on Homecoming. Offense and defense were rolling. Mark played like a "winner," and we are heading into the game against Cal next week playing for the Pac-10 Championship.

I dressed up as Tom Cruise from "Risky Business" last night and had a blast. And it would be safe to say that the town of Hermosa Beach got a hearty laugh at my white thighs.

Off to work, bro.

Miss ya and love ya, man,

Yogi

CAL

33

DATE: November 4, 2008
SUBJECT: Barack Obama

Ravi,

Today was the most important day of my life.

Tonight, I experienced the most profound 17 minutes of my life.

And January 20, 2009, will mark the most humble day in decades for our nation.

Barack Hussein Obama won the 2008 Presidential Election tonight. And he did it in a landslide.

And he accepted it ever so graciously.

In our office tonight, as I watched him offer his speech to the world, I, like many others, was brought to tears. And as I watched him speak so eloquently, I, like many others, swelled with pride.

But most important, as **President** Obama embraced the honor bestowed upon him, I, for the first time, found a living person other than a member of my family that I could call my idol, my hero.

As a child, teenager, and now young adult, I have looked up to people like Jordan, Rice, and Montana. I have always had an affinity for the stars of the past.

Leaders Bobby Kennedy, John Lennon, and, of course, Martin Luther King, Jr., were also on that short list for one reason: their profound impact on society. They truly changed society in a fashion that others deemed impossible, improbable, and ultimately dangerous. Their thoughts, ideals, and principles were so impactful that they actually led to naysayers wanting to take their lives, and of course, succeeding. Nonetheless, my heroes promoted a message heard round the world for decades, and still heard now.

That message: change is possible.

Although Bobby, John, and MLK stood on very different platforms on various social, political, and financial issues, they shared the stage when it came to common values regarding the human race. Values such as opportunity, curiosity, independence, and, most important, **love** led their respective movements. And they led fearlessly, ferociously, and humbly.

What I learned from them was that to be great, to be truly great, they had to be willing to risk their public persona because they could not let go of their independence, their message. None of my heroes ever forgot who he was, what he stood for, or where he was going.

While Obama's rhetoric was powerful, it was also full of grace. In fact, it was what he did **not** say that hit me the hardest.

After his speech, he stood on-stage next to Vice President Joe Biden. While Biden could only smile from ear to ear, Obama waved to the crowd as though he were in the 'zone' that only an athlete would know. He stood upon that stage as if to say, "I knew this night would happen, and I belong here." I watched him move about the stage, gazing into the crowd, and understood what it meant to be humble, honorable, and a world leader.

Today, Generation X received a role model, a leader comfortable enough to stand up for his personal beliefs, whether they concern health care, gay marriage, or the BCS system.

On January 20, 2009, Barack Hussein Obama will become our next President; he will re-energize the world's perception of America, as he exemplified that we should never to lose our ability to dream.

As we embark on the last 4 games of the year and our final push for a championship season, Barack Hussein Obama will become the Commander in Chief of the United States of America. He will change, impact, and challenge society all over again from the White House. And in our little world of college football, we will inspire, learn, and gain a greater understanding of culture as we try to do it better than it has ever been done before.

So, while we ball-out and Obama leads, I will promise you one thing: our squad will go for it this weekend vs. Cal and let it rip in the final month of this 2008-09 season.

Barack Hussein Obama, I thank you. I support you. And in a weird, universal way, our team, our staff, and we as individuals have learned a great deal from you.

Later bro,

Yogi

DATE: November 6, 2008
SUBJECT: Joe #7

#7 today…Am exhausted as we went out last night. John Glenn just moved out with his gal!

DATE: November 6, 2008
SUBJECT: Prop 8

Hey man,

Not sure if you heard yet, but California passed Proposition 8, which prohibits same-sex marriages. I don't really know what to say other than I'm sorry and I'm angry.

And it is a weird feeling, as I've never felt this angry before, this mad, this pissed off. I mean, who has the right to say who can and cannot spend their lives together? And in the world I live in currently, those who agree with me are few and far between.

But I will say that those close to me, who understand that this world does not need to revolve around a written word or its interpretation thousands of years ago, impress me with their thought processes.

I'm heading home as I'm pissed off, but I really do feel that at the end of the day, this will be overturned again.

Love ya, bro,

Yogi

P.S. How about the amount of history we are living right now? It's awesome!

DATE: November 7, 2008
SUBJECT: Friday Night

Ravi,

The only thing I could compare Friday night to is the moment before you step onstage. It is a night where all of our energies, all of our preparation, all of the time we put into our craft come together to form 1 heartbeat, 1 goal, 1 thought.

As Coach Carroll spoke tonight, I thought of how badly I want to be a head coach one day, and while all of the G.A. work sucks, it all proves worth it on Friday nights.

Hard to believe that there are only 2 games left at the Coliseum this season and likely in my career at USC.

Keep breaking a leg, man.

Miss ya,

Yogi

DATE: November 8, 2008
SUBJECT: Play-off Game

Ravi,

Just to remind you, this is a play-off game for us, as we are in a race to the finish. Our offense is playing well, but our defense has talent that is just off the charts. Gotta get Cal; they are well coached and have good athletes.

You better be watching!

Yogi

STANFORD

34

DATE: November 9, 2008
SUBJECT: October 6, 2007

Ravi,

Yes, October 6, 2007, was the night I never expected.
Yes, October 6, 2007, was the night you never expected.
Yes, October 6, 2007, was the night I couldn't sleep.

On that evening, over 13 months ago now, Stanford beat USC 24-23 in what is regarded as the largest upset in the history of college football.

I felt embarrassed, angry, repulsed, distraught, and shocked. And as I sit here thinking about that game and that night, those feelings have come rushing back like the Dalton creek after a storm.

Doubt I'll sleep much this week. We owe them one.

Yogi

P.S. We beat Cal 17-3.

DATE: November 11, 2008
SUBJECT: Revenge?

Ravi,

I know, I know, the e-mail I wrote the other night was an awkward one, as it was a weak moment. There will always be weak moments in our lives, but once we find them, it is up to us to deal with them productively. Thus, while our team and our staff surely want revenge and want to beat their ass this weekend, we can't afford to think that way.

Think about it, man, if our focus and energy are directed toward beating our opponent instead of preparing to play great, we will lose.

Winning, like acting in a show, is hard enough when you focus on your plays, or your lines. If you, or I, or our quarterback, tries too hard to focus on something out of our control, we will only put ourselves at a disadvantage.

So do we want revenge? Of course. What competitor wouldn't want to beat someone who got the best of them the previous time? But will we be driven by revenge? Not a chance. We are driven by the goal of playing Trojan football, playing focused, and playing physical.

Be sure to tune in, man!

Yogi

DATE: November 12, 2008
SUBJECT: T-shirt

Glenn called me today and reminded me of the t-shirt you had as a kid that read: "If Your Blood isn't Cardinal Red, You Need a Transfusion."

Hahahahaha.

Love ya, man! When are you coming to visit?

Yogi

DATE: November 14, 2008
SUBJECT: QB & Road Game

Ravi,

Game almost here and I can't tell you how excited I am to watch our quarterback play. He has learned a great deal about who he is this season and has figured out that at his core, he is a winner.

But since he has figured this out, we have played two home games. This will be the first real test for Mark as we head to the road—the first sell-out in Stanford's history. My feeling is that he and his philosophy will be tested, and if he truly knows who he is, then he will outlast any adversity.

Remember, if you figure out who you are and truly believe it, then there are *no choices*. You can't choose when to be a winner or when not to. You can't choose when to be a dreamer or when not to. You can't choose when to be a competitor or when not to.

If that's who you are, then you are that person 100% of the time. No choices, bro.

Love ya, pal,

Yogi

DATE: November 15, 2008
SUBJECT: Locker Room

45-23 was the final, and it sure feels great.

After being tied 17-17 at the half, we minimized our mistakes and out-physicaled them in the second half. While I have to give them credit, as they are much improved and headed in the right direction, this win feels as good as any all season.

Uncle Hank, Aunt Linda, and their kids came to the game after going to breakfast with me in the morning, so that was cool.

But as I sit here on the plane heading over the fires in southern California I must tell you that the locker room scene has stuck with me.

It wasn't especially flashy or full of uncommon exuberance, but it did hit me square between the eyes. I couldn't help but realize that we have only two regular season games left, not only in this season, but also, potentially, in my career at USC. And that thought is awkward.

I've never walked down a road that I knew was coming to an end, and as this season finishes up, I can sense the road narrowing. I know it's not the time to get emotional or reflective, but with a bye week on the horizon, a great team win in our rearview mirror, and most of the plane sleeping, I guess I can't help it.

Let's catch up tomorrow.

Miss ya and love ya, man,

Yogi

BYE WEEK

35

DATE: November 17, 2008
SUBJECT: Mom Retiring

Ravi,

We have a bye week. And during bye weeks we get to go home early, hang with our friends and family, and rejuvenate for the final stretch. For a GA, that means go out in Hermosa, go on a date (or two), and sleep in over the weekend.

Our last two games include Notre Dame and UCLA. The former I outwardly hate, after cheering for them as a child, and the latter ruined all of 2007 after beating us 13-9 on December 2, 2006. Currently, we are in position to share the Pac-10 Championship and go to a major bowl game, so it will be a blast as this pans out.

But much more important is Mom and what she did today in retiring from her job. A decision that had to be made and one that I hope she is glad that she made. It is easy to feel for her as she walks away from 13 years with the same company, away from 13 years of changing children's lives as an art therapist. But while neither you nor I can imagine walking away from a 13-year profession, we can learn something powerful from her.

It is, and always has been, Mom's desire to live her life on her own terms. While she is the first to admit that she had to deal with a lot of heartache at her job, she also dealt with joy. Today, she left with that happiness as she handed in her letter of resignation.

She is the one who made the choice to leave; she is the one who took ownership of her life.

Ravi—my opinion is that we often feel as though we don't have a choice in life, that we are stuck where we are working, living, and breathing. But, as you well know, that is not that case.

As Mom told us when we were young kids, "This is America—if you're not dreaming, then you're wrong. Dream impossible dreams and dare to be great."

And while this day was difficult for her, her children must learn from her as she proves once again that life is about choices and if we know who we are (like Mark and you are learning) then those choices become clear and simple. Bottom line—we are the ones who must live with our decisions, so we are the ones who must make them.

Wonder what she's doing today? What are you going to do on the day you retire? I'll probably go surfing.

Talk soon,

Yogi

DATE: November 20, 2008
SUBJECT: "You gotta put that in your book"

Ravi,

So today, when I was talking with Sark about how the season has gone by so fast, we started laughing about all of the stories we have. Then he said, about a particular one, which is totally not going in the book, "You've gotta put that in your book."

How classic was that.

We have tonight off. I'm headed out on a date.

Yogi

NOTRE DAME

36

DATE: November 24, 2008
SUBJECT: 24

Ravi,

Greatest show of all time on tonight—24. A 2-hour premier that the entire staff is jacked about. Our video guys recorded it, and I'm cruising home to sit on the couch and pretend I'm Jack Bauer (who I was for Halloween last year!)

Miss ya, bro,

Yogi

DATE: November 25, 2008
SUBJECT: Notre Dame

Ravi,

As you well know, Notre Dame was my dream school growing up, and I would have done anything to attend that prestigious university. When I was getting recruited, you, Dad, and I drove out to their summer camp hosted by their former head coach, Bob Davie.

Ronnie Rodamer and I were the two receivers competing for their one scholarship offer. Ronnie was 6'5," 210 lbs., and a beautiful athlete, while I was the 5'11," 180 pound scrapper with soft hands. While I thought I outperformed him, the staff at ND felt otherwise, and I was out of a scholarship to the Golden Dome.

But what you may not know is that the sole reason I went to Pitt was to get the chance to play Notre Dame three times. In fact, I took my visit to Pitt when they beat the Irish in the final game at Pitt Stadium.

Each year when we played them, I would dream about catching the game-winning touchdown pass at South Bend, and each year, that never happened. But while I never had a reception versus the Irish, I can remember every snap I took on that 3-inch-thick grass field.

This week will be another special experience, as it may very well be my final game against the Irish and my final in the historic Los Angeles Memorial Coliseum.

Hope you get to check it out.

Love ya, pal,

Yogi

Date: November 26, 2008
Subject: Rain

May rain this weekend. It is pouring right now at 11:39 PM as I sit at my office desk staring out the small window in front of me.

Not a big deal, but there are many issues this week that could take our focus away from the game at hand: the rain, the future of Charlie Weis (ND's head coach), and the futures of our own staff members. You see, the next two months will be key as coaches will move from job to job and there will be opportunities for young guys like me to move to another team. But, as I learned two years ago when the Raiders thing went down, I can't control any of those outside issues.

Kind of like if you have a show—you cannot control how many people attend, if the lighting is good or bad, if the speakers work well or not, etc. All you can do is prepare to give a great performance and let everything else fall into place.

Weird that looking at the rain out of my small window inspired this e-mail....

Talk soon,

Yogi

DATE: November 27, 2008
SUBJECT: Happy Thanksgiving

Hey man,

Happy Thanksgiving! Break a leg tonight! I know Mom and Dad are heading to your show. Thanksgiving is always a good time as we get to hang with friends, eat good food, and reflect on what we are thankful for.

As I sit here, I'm first and foremost thankful for you, man, my best friend. You've kept going for it and have never stopped dreaming—you're the man, bro!

Also, as I approach my final game in the Coliseum, I can't help but think about how thankful I am to have been here for the past 4 seasons, to have lost only 1 game in the Coli during that stretch, and to have been around so many amazing people.

It's gonna be different on Saturday, as I know it's likely my final time in that stadium, final time on that field for pre-game, and final time giving the Fight On salute to the band from the floor of the Coliseum…but different is good, and who knows which sideline I'll be on next fall.

Off to Glenn's for dinner.

Love ya, and give Mom and Dad a hug from LA,

Yogi

DATE: November 28, 2008
SUBJECT: Friday Night

Ravi,

So it's Friday night again—the best night of the football season. In his speech tonight, Coach Carroll talked about playing our final game at the Coliseum and how we have reached the goal of our season.

Before the first game we talked about how the goal for our team in 2008-09 would be to find out who we are, and that there would be a Friday night during the season when we would figure that out.

Tonight, we did.

We are physical, we are poised, and we are badass. We play with great energy, great enthusiasm, great toughness and we play smart. We are authentic. And that is enough to dominate tomorrow, because we know who we are, bro. Now, we can go to sleep knowing that tomorrow evening when we hit the field at 5:08 PM, we have earned the right to let it rip and truly go for it on every snap.

Yogi

P.S. We had a few guys outside of the program sit in on the team meeting tonight. I wish I could tell you how proud it makes us feel to hear them describe what we do.

DATE: November 30, 2008
SUBJECT: Don't want to go to sleep

It's 2:33 AM and I don't want to go to sleep, bro, because I know that when I close my eyes and pass out, this night will end. And on this night, we beat Notre Dame 38-3.

The beautiful thing about sports is that we love them for the special moments that they create, and we also never want those moments to end. I guess I don't want to pass out because I know that there is only 1 more regular season game left in my coaching career at SC.

In a text message today, you asked why it was so, and the answer is: it's just the profession. You coach a few seasons, then move on to a new program, a new team, a new culture... and of course, a new adventure.

Yogi

P.S. The celebration was awesome as Hermosa Beach toasted to the Golden Dome into the evening.

UCLA

37

DATE: December 1, 2008
SUBJECT: Coaching Carousel

Ravi,

Every year around this time the coaching carousel begins, and that means that guys leave jobs and take jobs. A circus, as it can drive a young coach crazy, but also very exciting.

Lane Kiffin, the old Raiders coach and the man who taught me offensive football at USC during my first two seasons and mentored me, just took the Tennessee job. There are also a few other coaching openings around the country that get me jacked up, but then I wake up at the beach, look at the sets of waves rolling in, and realize that, at 27 years of age, I value where I live more than where I work, regardless of how good an 'opportunity' may look to others.

Am thinking about walking away from coaching…let's talk when you can.

Love ya, man,

Yogi

DATE: December 2, 2008
SUBJECT: Competition Tuesday

Today was the last "Competition Tuesday" of the regular season, and while I'm tired from the wear and tear of a long season, I can admit that I'll miss this next fall.

Not trying to get reflective just yet, but the reality is setting in.

How's life, bro?

Yogi

DATE: December 3, 2008
SUBJECT: Joe # 8

Had cup number 8 today. Looks like I'll remain under 10. Kicking traditional coaching methods' ass!!!

Hope all is well.

Yogi

Date: December 4, 2008
Subject: Washington and Sark

So Sark is going to get the head coaching job at Washington. I'm so proud of him, as he has worked so hard and is so deserving of it. On one hand I wish he were staying at USC, as I think he'll be the next head coach here, but I would probably do the same thing as him, since the opportunity to lead a team and change a culture is too good to pass up.

That said, he asked me to join him as his QB coach. A HUGE opportunity: Washington is a major program, and their QB is one of the best in the nation. A no-brainer, right? But I'm not sure.

I have another opportunity here in LA to do some cool stuff. I'll be able to cultivate creative ideas and at the same time stay around ball.

So here we sit, Thursday evening, after what may be my final regular season practice as a ball coach, and two options are sitting in front of me. Continue to coach or get back into the broadcasting/analyst field.

So I'm going to tell myself what I would tell you: Relax and enjoy the next two days and the final regular season game vs. UCLA, and then head to the beach on Sunday and gather all of the information on both jobs. Then sit down on my board, paddle into a few waves, and just listen.

Love ya, man,

Yogi

DATE: December 5, 2008
SUBJECT: Friday Night

Ravi,

Coach Carroll's message was simple tonight: Enjoy tomorrow. Enjoy the moments. Enjoy your teammates. Enjoy this game we love.

So simple, yet so true.

And as my final game as a USC Trojan comes to a close, I cannot lie, bro, and say that it won't be hard, but I can also say with full confidence that I'll take a look around the Rose Bowl, soak in the atmosphere, and be sure not to miss a thing.

I love ya, man,

Yogi

DATE: December 6, 2008
SUBJECT: Rose Bowl

We got Penn State in the Rose Bowl. While I think we would beat any of the teams ranked in front of us, this match-up couldn't be more perfect. Final game at USC, possible final game coaching…and it is against the team I grew up hating with all my heart.

Hope you can make it.

Yogi

THE COACHING CAROUSEL

38

DATE: December 8, 2008
SUBJECT: Advice

Ravi,

Went for the SC quarterbacks job today harder than I've ever gone for anything. I told Coach Carroll that I earned it, was prepared for it, and quite honestly deserved it. And he agreed. But then he went on to say that while he felt my coaching the QBs was the best thing for our team, he didn't feel it was the best thing for our staff. Reason being, we have a young staff, and he wants them to have a guy around who can basically oversee the entire operation. While I understand that and almost agree with it from an advisory standpoint, I am obviously pissed and disagree from my standpoint.

As you know, Sark has offered me the QB job at Washington. Seattle is a cool city, and Sark is practically family to me, but I just don't know if I want to make that move. It's kind of funny, but during my first year, he and I were out at dinner, and he told me that we would be coaching at Washington together someday.

Who would've known?

Also, Los Angeles offers opportunities like no other city, other than the one you're living in, so I could stay here and dive back into the broadcast/entertainment world.

Who knows, but it's good to have options.

Talk later,

Yogi

DATE: December 10, 2008
SUBJECT: Decision

So, as you already know, I have a decision to make with two options. I found out the financials today on both, and they are relatively equal and relatively more than I've made combined in 4 years at USC. I'm telling ya, man, I'm really torn.

Need to surf.

Love and miss ya,

Yogi

Date: December 11, 2008
Subject: Advice

Hey son,

Good to talk to you the other evening. As you know, Mom is concerned about the fast lane in Hollywood and wants only the best for you. She worries about things and wants you to be careful in your choices. She knows what it feels like to be 'in-between' and means the best.

Life choices are funny: you get a feel and you catch one wave while you let others go by. Some waves never come back, or if they do, they won't be the same, so enjoy and savor the moment.

It's the choices not made that you regret more than the ones made (kind of interesting here). But remember that new directions offer new possibilities.

Watch out for promises as they can bring darkness and interrupt the flow of light. Those promises can be quite seductive, and if you are not resolute in resisting them, the moment can be lost to misfortune.

Examine your motives. Any questionable motives need to be rooted out and discarded.

Use your higher nature to test the rightness of things. Watch out for situations that tempt your ego and tempt you into anger, righteousness, or desire. That which seems suspicious almost certainly is.

Be modest, independent, and patient with great discipline.

Avoid arrogance and anger at all costs.

Be balanced. When you are around unknown circumstances, withdraw into stillness.

On a positive note: practice kindness, humility, correctness, and openness.

Be open with all relationships so that all facets are seen as fair and correct by everyone concerned, not just yourself.

Don't have or continue to have relationships with unspoken reservations or hidden intentions.

When you have a fellowship with enlightened people, exceptional things can happen.

Yogi, be sageful (look that one up).

Meet others halfway in a spirit of sincerity and receptiveness.

Give trust where due. Where it is not, do not resort to harshness.

Avoid forming factions and cliques, and correct errors in relationships as soon as you become aware of them.

By doing the above you can accomplish magnificent deeds now.

Hidden intentions or agendas of the ego prevent proper fellowship. Misfortune results when unity and truth are ignored.

So cling to what is correct/right and meet in the open without ambitions.

Good luck.

Love, Dad

P.S. Keep us posted.

DATE: December 12, 2008
SUBJECT: Re: Advice

Dad—

Thanks for the advice. This decision will be easier than the Oakland one, which is cool. Miss you, will call later, and tell Mom what up.

Yogi

P.S. – looked up sageful. Not a word, Dad. But thanks for getting me to the dictionary. Knowledge is no burden to carry.

DATE: December 14, 2008
SUBJECT: Decision

Ravi,

I'm staying in LA. Staying in Hermosa Beach. Staying in the land where dreams come true.

While it can be considered risky, crazy, or just plain stupid to turn down a full-time coaching position at a major Division I school for more money than Mom or Dad ever made, I have to follow the truths laid down by our parents.

I can vividly recall being about 5 years old and Mom kneeling down with me in our backyard on that big rock. She grasped both my tiny hands, brushed away my hair, and looked me in the eye.

"Yogi, your name was given to you for a reason. You need to have balance within your mind, body, and soul…so dream big and remember that if you're not dreaming, you're wrong."

As I got older, she would often go back to that moment and discuss things such as the United States and how it meant so much to her parents. When she arrived from Israel, she and her family knew that they had landed in a country where opportunity lived and the "American Dream" flourished. So, tonight, before I went to the fireworks show in Manhattan Beach with a few friends, I called Sark and told him that I had to give all of my dreams a shot. And like a best friend would do, he was jacked and supported my decision.

Not sure how many close friends you have in NYC, but be sure to appreciate the ones you do have because they are truly special, as Sark is that to me.

Rock on, bro!

Yogi

P.S. We'll have to fly out to Seattle on your private jet and watch Sark win the Pac-10 title when you hit the Hollywood screen!

ROSE BOWL

39

DATE: December 15, 2008
SUBJECT: Phone Call

Ravi,

Sark called last night and it was awesome. We talked about his staff, his team, and the energy around his program. I'm so proud of him and excited for his new staff.

Talking with him was one of the coolest experiences of my life—I was so relaxed. I thought there would be a large part of me wanting to be there, but only about 2% of me was thinking about being a Husky. So all in all, it was a great feeling, as I knew that my decision was the right one.

Keep ballin' out in your show!

Yogi

DATE: December 16, 2008
SUBJECT: Colin Cowherd

Was driving in today when I heard Colin Cowherd on the radio talking about Sark and other assistant coaches who are leaving their bowl-bound teams to become head coaches. His premise was that these coordinators and new head coaches would not focus on their bowl games because they have so many other things on their minds.

I couldn't disagree more! These guys are so successful precisely because of their ability to multi-task and when it comes down to game-planning, it becomes relaxing to focus **only** on ball.

So while I'm typically a big fan of Colin Cowherd, today I would have to disagree with Mom's favorite radio show.

Rip it, man,

Yogi

DATE: December 17, 2008
SUBJECT: Last of Everything

Ravi,

Hard to believe, but starting today every day of practice is the "final" one of its kind. Crazy, bro.

Let's get it!

Yogi

DATE: December 20, 2008
SUBJECT: Charr and Speech

So this guy Charr Gahagan, one of our strength coaches, is leaving to go with Sark after the Rose Bowl. Today he spoke to the boys—said he wanted to get something off his chest. And it was a very cool moment.

After he began with a simple "thank you," his eyes welled up, and his voice cracked.

But as he continued, he spoke of how our players listen to various speakers each year who often talk of competition, perseverance, toughness, and hard work. But Charr said he wanted to talk about a different quality, one that he felt encompassed them all. He walked to the whiteboard behind him, took out a red marker, and wrote in large capital letters: "L-O-V-E."

He told us how he felt that the simple concept of "LOVE" can allow someone to live freely, live happily, and live purposefully.

He then took that thick red marker and wrote another word on the board: "AGAPE."

As you may or may not know, agape means unconditional love. Charr basically said that if you live with "Agape Love," then you love others unconditionally.

As he continued, he spoke of his favorite Bible verse. It went something like this: "I owe no man anything except one thing: To love him."

Now you have to picture Charr. He is about 5'8", 210 lbs., and rocked up. The national power lifting champion in America three times, he finished as high as third in the world at one point. And he is as Southern as anyone I know. So imagine this short, jacked Southern guy talking about "Agape Love" to 105 football players. It was awesome!

As he continued, he spoke of how he is challenged in his job at times. Whether a player gives him attitude or a coach refuses to remain in the coaches' box on the sideline during a game, Charr said he often gets frustrated, as he is just trying to do his job. But when he does get upset, he told us, he prays. Each time he asks God about what he should do, and the good Lord tells him you need to "Love him anyway!"

How cool is it that this strength coach, who has not said more than 10 words in a row in my four years at USC, just gave a powerful and relatively spiritual speech to our team with the core message being that, to succeed in life, you need to live with "Agape Love."

It's crazy: as this thing is winding down and every day really is the last of its kind, I keep thinking about all the special people that this program has in it and how lucky we are to have one another.

Talk soon, man. Miss ya, bro.

Yogi

DATE: December 23, 2008
SUBJECT: What a Year

Tonight the entire crew is heading out on the town, and for good reason. Jared and Ivan are moving to Seattle to work at Washington, and our friend, Andy, just got engaged. As you might imagine, we will be toasting throughout the evening.

As I sit here in my apartment waiting to hop in a cab, I can't help but reflect on the power of football and the pageantry of a season. Each season truly is a lifetime...

Andy moves back to Hermosa and gets engaged to his beautiful bride-to-be, Laura; Brennan is on the verge of having a child with Amber; Glenn moves out to LA; Sark gets a dream job in Seattle; Jared gets a much-deserved raise; Ivan becomes the new head strength and conditioning coach of the Huskies; we finish 11-1 in the regular season; and I get to coach my final game against Penn State—the team I grew up reading about.

Can you even imagine all of those things happening in the span of 5 months?

It's the beauty of ball, the pageantry of sport, and the authenticity of life…and it's the holiday season. What more can you ask for?

Miss ya and love ya, bro!

Yogi

DATE: December 25, 2008
SUBJECT: Christmas

Merry Christmas! I know you are all having a blast in New York City, and I would expect nothing less. I wish I could be there and hang with the family, but it's all good—we'll see each other soon, bro.

Am about to go surfing (a Christmas morning tradition the past four years), grab a bite to eat, and just relax.

Am fired up for this game and can't wait until it gets here. I feel like most of Pennsylvania is coming out to watch as well.

Talk soon, man. Love ya and give everyone a hug.

And break a leg tonight, pal!

Yogi

DATE: December 26, 2008
SUBJECT: Penn State game

Hey man,

So this will be a physical game as Penn State was 1 point away from being undefeated. They are not the typical Big 10 team since they have speed, size, and the schemes to beat us. Should be an interesting game—they are much better than Illinois last year.

Talk later,

Yogi

DATE: December 27, 2008
SUBJECT: Final Competition Tuesday

Ravi,

Coach Carroll spoke about how today, the final "Competition Tuesday," is huge: to beat Penn State on New Year's Day, we first have to beat them today. So we, like you in your show tonight, have to bring it and compete all day long.

Yogi

DATE: December 27, 2008
SUBJECT: Soccer and friends from PA

Hey man,

Practiced on the soccer field as our field is torn apart from the rain last week. Also, friends from home like Jim Coles from Channel 16, Coach Jack Henzes and Coach Greg Dolhon, along with their families were at practice, which was awesome. Lastly, LA is flooded with blue and white as it looks like the Pennsylvania craze has entered Southern California!

I'm out. And the Penn State blue and white is making me nauseous.

Yogi

DATE: January 2, 2008
SUBJECT: Joe

I think I'm off the joe altogether. Been a month since cup #8....

Love ya, bro,

Yogi

DATE: December 29, 2008
SUBJECT: Brennan

Today is the final "No Turnover Wednesday" practice of my coaching career. It is also the final time I'll drive to and from work with Brennan.

Not a big deal on the surface, but one that really hits me.

The commute to work can easily be overlooked, but in LA it has two purposes: 1) the carpool factor and 2) the ride home.

Over the past four years, Brennan and I have met around 7:00 each morning. When we begin our drive on the Pacific Coast Highway, he puts his sunglasses on and turns up the music while I read the sports section of the *LA Times* and attempt to take a quick nap.

But around 11:00 PM, on the drive home, we not only catch up on the day's activities but also talk about everything—our players, relationships, jobs, kids, life, etc. It's been these 22 groundhog-like minutes on the way home from Heritage Hall that have aided me through countless days, weeks, and ultimately, four football seasons.

Loyal to a fault, Brennan is a rare individual. Like our early, sleep-deprived rides into work and our late, conversation-filled races home, he has remained genuine.

So, on our final night on the freeways of LA, I must say that I'll miss these cruises for two reasons: 1) the carpool factor and 2) the ride home.

Talk soon, as it's almost here,

Yogi

DATE: December 30, 2008
SUBJECT: I am in love with Joe Paterno

Ravi,

Yes, the text message I sent was correct: I am in love with Joe Paterno.

Tonight, our staff had dinner with Penn State's in Los Angeles at a very cool venue. As dinner was starting, I began to search for a seat. None were available, so I sat at a table alone.

When I returned from getting a plate of food from the buffet, I noticed that Coach Joe Paterno was sitting at my table. Assuming he had an entourage with him, I asked if he wanted me to leave.

He snapped back, "No, you're sitting right here. What's your name, son?"

At that moment, I fell in love with Joe Paterno.

For the next ninety minutes, I ate dinner with JoPa, his wife, Coach Carroll, Coach's wife, and a few others. But this was not an ordinary dinner. JoPa was asking me questions about Dalton, PA, busting my chops about Pitt, and having a blast with the entire table.

I have to tell you, I was so impressed with how sharp he was, how witty he was, and how genuine he was. I never thought this would come out of my mouth, or my fingers on this computer, but I am in love with Joe Paterno.

Yogi

P.S. I hope the Pitt faithful don't hate me. Remember, I said I love Joe Paterno, not "I love Penn State!"

DATE: December 31, 2008
SUBJECT: Joe Pa's press conference

So how about this, bro. Today at JoPa's press conference, I guess he was asked about our staff. And he said, "Yogi Roth will be a great head coach someday."

How about that! (Sorry, but I'm going to enjoy this moment.)

DATE: December 31, 2008
SUBJECT: The Final Friday Night

Ravi,

As you know, Friday nights are my favorite part of this game that I have grown to cherish. And as you also know, this was my final Friday night as a USC Trojan.

While I sat in the team room, I wished you were sitting by my side and just feeling it, too. Feeling our energy, enthusiasm, confidence, trust, focus, and the "knowing" that we will dominate Penn State tomorrow afternoon on college football's most historic stage, the Rose Bowl in Pasadena.

Tonight, Coach Carroll spoke of how this was our final "teachable moment." The lesson taught was not to change, regardless of the hype and no matter the circumstances.

So, on New Year's Eve, in a downtown LA hotel, as we come to a close regarding our final preparations for the 2009 Rose Bowl, it is time just to live the *Win Forever* philosophy, because that is who we are, and that will *always* be enough.

Ravi—In my final "teachable moment" to you, my best friend since we grew up in PA, I leave you with the same message. When you arrive on Broadway and have a clear vision of who you are and what you stand for—know that your mentality will always be enough.

You will be the actor who knows his role and lives it, the actor who masters his role and performs it, and the brother who sets his dream and actualizes it.

Love ya, man.

Yogi

DATE: January 2, 2008
SUBJECT: Still haven't slept

Ravi,

We won 38-24, in dominant fashion. I still haven't fallen asleep because once I do, I will wake up no longer a coach.

But as I yawn in front of my laptop, I also know that I'll wake up and the language of the world will be screaming at me to live life, be curious, and compete at a new normal while at peace.

Thanks for coming along for the ride and thanks for listening. I'm off to the beach.

Yogi

EPILOGUE

PATHETIC?

Okay, maybe not so much. You be the judge.

The life lived, the lessons learned—it's in your hands now. Do with it what you will.

And let's be serious, there is no reason under the sun that a 26-year-old kid should be offering up stories of his life and realistically thinking that others will read about them. But I do.

Why?

I guess it would be because I have gone through the process of figuring out who I am and what I stand for. From birth, I have been influenced by uncommon and unique people who have challenged me and inspired me to dream. Those dreams have led me to journeys throughout the world, and I've been given the opportunity to fall in love with foreign countries, different cultures, the vast array of humanity, and of course, football.

The basic concepts I grew up with were "good things always happen to good people" and "hard work always pays off." They have carried me since I was dribbling a basketball on the Dalton Courts. Are they truths? Doubtful. Are they absolutes? Depends on how you spin it.

But maybe that's the beauty of those competitive thoughts—they can be spun, just like anything inside our minds. We have the power, we control the message, we choose how we think, we choose how we react, and we choose how we move forward. Some are conscious decisions; some unconscious. But all are ours—entirely.

Which may lead to a question still unanswered, "Why can't you keep coaching the game you love? Why walk away from the greatest job in the world?"

The easy answer is that there is not enough room on USC's staff, and I do not want to live anywhere else in the country. The more attractive reason is that I am choosing lifestyle over profession, the beach over money. The true reason lies somewhere in between—and within the pages of this book.

From PA to LA isn't a story that will change the world (as I said at the outset, "I'm pathetic"). Nonetheless, it is a story that we all write—those of us in small towns with big dreams, and those in big cities who shape their futures on crowded streets. No matter what, no matter where, we all create the visions by which we live. We all must travel, within ourselves and perhaps around the world. We all must find our places, and we all must discover our names. We need follow no predetermined paths—only the rules we set, the styles we choose, and the competitiveness with which we approach new challenges. Each challenge is different, whether it be as straightforward as trying to make varsity as a freshman, coach football, or write a book. Or as complex as leaving a job, ending a relationship, or moving your life across the country. Maybe the challenges will force us to chase a dream. Or, perhaps, they will require us to let go of one.

But whatever decisions each of us make, whatever journeys each of us take, they are ours: our paths to forge and our stories to write. Each of us has a past—both individual and collective—to recover, a present to understand, and a future to build.

So, as I end one trip and begin another, I thank you for reading, and I ask you this one thing: find your story, live it, and tell it.

I'll be listening.

Acknowledgments

IF YOU'VE READ THIS BOOK, YOU'RE PART OF MY STORY. And if you're in it, I am honored by your presence.

But there are many others who've contributed—some in ways small yet significant, others in ways profound and life-transforming. The first person who inspired this was Sarah Banet-Weiser, my professor at USC. She supported the concept and offered advice like a good friend would. Also, the first set of eyes to read and offer edits to this book were those of Adriane Stewart, whose advice and questions forced me to understand the goal of these pages.

As this book developed, there were many little aspects I hadn't considered. Some were simple like a cover and a title, and some complex like the formatting, but without the help of photographer DeWalt Mix, graphic designer Brad Vinson, and KMD Publishing, this would have not become something we can now hold in our hands. Furthermore, the advice, support and friendship from Elizabeth Hayes and E-Communications Group was off the charts—thank you.

But I would be remiss if I did not state clearly who this book reflects. Sure, my friends from Dalton, Pitt, USC and beyond, have influenced me, but the book's underlying theme originated because of every youth, high school and college coach I have ever met, and there are many of you. As I wrote this book, I was finding myself laughing about lay-up drills with Coach Brian Heffron and others; my first coaching gig at 14 years old with Dave Maddock and our 5th grade basketball team; and of course, the day the three boys from Dalton met Tom Parry, who would become not only our high school basketball coach, but lifelong friend. As I got older, I met Curt Sohns in eighth grade and T.J. Fadden in ninth, where they gave me the chance of a lifetime while introducing me to the love of my young life—my helmet, pads, and football. From there, the entire Gerry, Jeff and Scot Wasilchak family and their staff honed my game on the field, and developed in me a competitive mentality that inspires my life to this day. In college, it was not just Coach Harris or Coach Brookhart, but Paul Rhoads—whose passion reminded me often how fortunate we were to be a part of the game of football.

And now that I'm in L.A., thousands of miles from the Dalton Courts and Lackawanna Trail, the team and coaching staff I am surrounded by can only be described in one word—epic. Pete Carroll, Keith Sarkisian, Andy Bark, Dave Perron, Gary Uberstine, Michael Gale, Michael Fountain, Su-zAnn Brantner, Peter Ruppe, Matt Rhoades, Bob Best, Ron Meridith, Jordan Meridith, Jared Blank, Shervin Mirhashemi, Kevin Smith, Tim Tessalone, E.J. Borghetti, Pete Donaldson, and more, as well as up and coming leaders like Sarah Fish, Will Roth, Allegra Roth, Brendan Roth, Anna Roth, Jane Roth, Benjamin Roth, Theo Brendan Norbert Debus, Kevin Jackson, Connor Smith, Dillon Carroll, Malia Tamilin, Slader Bark, Justen Ruppe, Jillian Irwin, Jesse Irwin, Ricky Rosas, and Jake Olson inspire me daily. Thank you as you all force me to dream and hold me accountable to those affirmations.

Also, the constant support and belief from Adam Gelvan, Josh Pyatt, Jeff Shumway, Glen Mastroberte, Cher Van Amburg, Jeremy Katz, Josh Mervis and their teams drive my desire to perform each day. To all of you—many thanks and many things to come.

And to the one who challenges my every thought and won't allow me to back off my dreams for a moment—Mark Jackson—you have no idea, man. The countless phone calls, the endless advice and the many laughs are more appreciated than you know. How you have stood tall in my corner all these years makes me extremely fortunate. Love ya man.

Pete Carroll, you have been there as a boss, surfer, co-author, and mentor. But throughout the past eight years, you have constantly been a friend. From late night calls to early morning e-mails and mid-day texts you have supported every endeavor I've had, unlike anyone outside my family. You encouraged my often uncommon thinking and supported my often unsafe jaunts into the West Bank, South America or India. Yet the common theme is that you challenged me to continue to dream and to never settle. For that, and that alone, thanks, Coach.

Special thanks to my publishers, Jim Kowatch and Chris DeLuca. Your tireless encouragement (and flexibility regarding deadlines) made this enjoyable as KMD Publishing takes off. And the fact that we are all Pitt grads makes it even sweeter. Well done and Hail to Pitt.

And finally, the person who embodies the phrase "Always Compete" more than anyone I know, Bob Bancroft. To edit this entire manuscript was a massive

project, but to do it with a tireless work ethic, constant smile and upbeat enthusiasm was well, you know, somewhat impressive for a guy who's primarily
an actor. Thanks bro. You're the man.

And thank you all—to those of you mentioned and those of you who are
not. This page could go on forever, but regardless of the names in print or the
stories told—your impact, inspiration, competitiveness and love mean more
than you could possibly imagine. So as I bid this manuscript adieu, thank you
and keep dreamin'.

Thank you, football.
Thank you, friends.
Thank you, family.
Thank you, heroes.
Thank you, Friday nights.
Thank you, Saturday afternoons.
Thank you, Pete and Brennan.
Thank you, PA and LA.
Thank you, readers.